HITTITE FORTIFICATIONS
c.1650–700 BC

KONSTANTIN S NOSSOV

ILLUSTRATED BY BRIAN DELF

Series editors Marcus Cowper and Nikolai Bogdanovic

D1026999

First published in Great Britain in 2008 by Osprey Publishing,
Midland House, West Way, Botley, Oxford OX2 0PH, United Kingdom
443 Park Avenue South, New York, NY 10016, USA
Email: info@ospreypublishing.com

A CIP catalogue record for this book is available from the British Library.

ISBN 978 1 84603 207 3

Editorial by Ilios Publishing, Oxford, UK (www.iliospublishing.com)
Page layout by Ken Vail Graphic Design, Cambridge, UK (kvgd.com)
Typeset in Sabon and Myriad Pro
Index by Alison Worthington
Maps by The Map Studio Ltd, Romsey, Hants.
Originated by PPS Grasmere, Leeds, UK
Printed and bound in China through Bookbuilders

08 09 10 11 12   10 9 8 7 6 5 4 3 2 1

FOR A CATALOGUE OF ALL BOOKS PUBLISHED BY OSPREY MILITARY
AND AVIATION PLEASE CONTACT:

NORTH AMERICA
Osprey Direct, c/o Random House Distribution Center, 400 Hahn Road,
Westminster, MD 21157
Email: info@ospreydirect.com

ALL OTHER REGIONS
Osprey Direct UK, PO Box 140, Wellingborough,
Northants, NN8 2FA, UK
Email: info@ospreydirect.co.uk

www.ospreypublishing.com

DEDICATION

To Andrew Sarjevsky, my true friend and loyal companion in far from easy
expeditions in Asia Minor.

ACKNOWLEDGEMENTS

The author wishes to express sincere thanks to Vladimir Golubev who
created the black and white images for this book.

Special thanks are due to Mustafa Metin, archaeologist in the Museum
of Ancient Civilizations in Ankara who kindly advised the author on the
dating of artefacts preserved in the museum.

The author also thanks Murat Bektas, the guide who took us about the ruins
of Hattusha, Alacahöyük and Yazilikaya and revealed not only an excellent
knowledge of the sites but also great patience while we examined the ruins.

AUTHOR'S NOTE

The spelling of proper nouns and geographical names in the book is
as close to the original as possible. One exception has only been made
for the city of Hattusha, which is commonly known by this name but
is also encountered as Hattuša or Hattuşaş, as well as in its Hattian form
Hattus/Hattush. Unfortunately, the original Hittite names of many of the
sites are unknown to us today. And these sites are named after the closest
modern Turkish settlement. The following rules should be born in mind in
reading Turkish names:

Turkish c is read j (for instance, in Alacahöyük)
Turkish ç is read ch (for instance, in Içel)
Turkish ğ is read gh (for instance, in Boğazköy)
Turkish ş is read sh (for instance, in Alişar)
The letter š that occurs often in the names of Hittite kings is written
either as sh or as s.

All the photographs in this book are from the author's collection.
All requests should be addressed to: konst-nosov@mtu-net.ru
or konstantin_nossov@yahoo.com.

ARTIST'S NOTE

Readers may care to note that the original paintings from which the
colour plates in this book were prepared are available for private sale.
All reproduction copyright whatsoever is retained by the Publishers.
All enquiries should be addressed to:

Brian Delf
7 Burcot Park
Burcot
Abingdon
Oxon
OX14 3DH
UK

The Publishers regret that they can enter into no correspondence upon
this matter.

THE FORTRESS STUDY GROUP (FSG)

The object of the FSG is to advance the education of the public in the
study of all aspects of fortifications and their armaments, especially
works constructed to mount or resist artillery. The FSG holds an annual
conference in September over a long weekend with visits and evening
lectures, an annual tour abroad lasting about eight days, and an annual
Members' Day.
The FSG journal FORT is published annually, and its newsletter Casemate
is published three times a year. Membership is international. For further
details, please contact:

The Secretary, c/o 6 Lanark Place, London W9 1BS, UK
website: www.fsgfort.com

GLOSSARY

ašandula/i-	Garrison
gurta-	Fortress
gurtawanni-	A castellan, an inhabitant or defender of a fortress; the term has only recently been come across and its meaning is unclear
höyük (hüyük)	Turkish word for a mound of a typical archaeological site formed by debris of an ancient settlement (usually prior to the Classical Period). Such mounds are particularly high where there was a number of mainly mud-brick settlements built successfully on one and the same place. Mud-brick cannot be used twice, so when old buildings became redundant, the site was leveled out and new buildings built on top. Thus, layer by layer an artificial mound grew. Turkish höyük is similar to Arabic *tell*, Hebrew *tel* and Persian *tepe*.
kârum	'Port' in Akkadian, although its meaning was extended to refer to any Assyrian merchant colony whether it bordered water or not.

CONTENTS

HITTITE FORTIFICATIONS
*c.*1650–700 BC

INTRODUCTION

In the second half of the 3rd millennium BC the Indo-European tribes known to us as the Hittites started to migrate to and settle in Central Anatolia. At that time it was a land of small city-states some of whose names have survived to this day, such as Kaneš (Neša), Kuššara, Hattusha, Zalpa and Puruskhanda; however, the exact location of these sites is not always known. The newcomers gradually settled all over Central Anatolia and took control of the region. The merging of the Hittites with the indigenous Hattian population appears to have been a fairly peaceful process, though some armed conflict is indicated by traces of destruction in strata from the period discovered at Alacahöyük, Ališar, Hattusha and others.

A distinct Hittite culture emerged as the result of several centuries of merging of Hattian and Indo-European traditions. So, while the Hattian language was ousted by that of the newcomers, it was not forgotten and was later used by Hittite priests in performing some of the rites. Moreover, the Hittite state was known throughout Mesopotamia as the 'Land of Hatti'.

The first recorded Hittite kings are Pithana and Anitta who ruled from the as yet undiscovered city of Kuššara. Later, Anitta removed the capital to Neša, and the Hittites began to call their language Neshian after that city. Anitta

Sam'al (Zincirli): general plan of fortifications and the reconstructed south city gate. The urban fortifications formed a circle and consisted of a double wall with 100 towers and three gates. The southern gate was most formidable one: in addition to the gates in the outer and inner walls it had a low fortification (barbican) in front. Each of the three gates was strengthened with two flanking towers projecting forward.

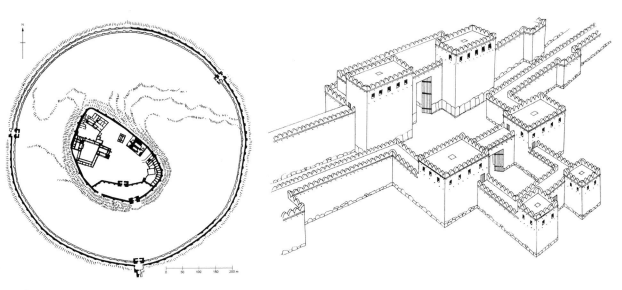

The space between the inner and outer walls on the Yerkapi Rampart in Hattusha. The outer wall was erected towards the end of the 13th century BC, probably in the face of a growing threat to the city. The wall blocked the flights of steps on both sides of the rampart and the Sphinx Gate in the middle. The towers of the outer wall were put in between the towers of the main wall.

was a great conqueror who subjugated the city-states of Neša, Zalpa and Puruskhanda, as well as destroying Hattusha and anathematizing it for all time, threatening anyone who settled there with the wrath of the Weather God. One of his successors, however, did not heed the curse and in mid-17th century BC removed the capital from Kuššara (where it had moved back to from Neša) to Hattusha. He took the name of Hattušili or 'one from Hattusha'. Hattušili I is considered to be the founder of the Old Hittite Kingdom and he, along with his successor Muršili I, subjugated large territories not only in Central Anatolia but also in Syria and Mesopotamia. Muršili I even captured Babylon in 1595 BC, thus causing the downfall of the First Babylonian Dynasty. The largest external threat to the Hittite Kingdom during this period was the Hurrian Kingdom of the Mitanni (located in what is today the south-east of Turkey and the northern parts of Syria and Iraq). Hurrian raids led to the secession of some of the southern and eastern Anatolian provinces from the Hittites, and may well have been the spur that led to the rapid development of the art of fortification in the region. The Old Kingdom period witnesses the appearance of cyclopean fortification walls, hitherto unknown in Anatolia. Hantili I (c.1590–60 BC) in particular rebuilt and strengthened the fortifications of the city of Hattusha.

A period of internal unrest only ended with the accession to the throne of Telipinu (c.1525 BC) and, by the reign of Šuppiluliuma I (c.1380–40 BC), the Hittite Kingdom reached its prime. Šuppiluliuma I, along with his successors Muršili II and Muwatalli II, made the Hittite Empire one of the leading powers of the ancient Near East. As a result of military operations or carefully thought-out treaties, the Hittites subjected the western regions of Asia Minor, the kingdom of the Mitanni and Syria as far north as the river Euphrates to their rule. This expansion led to conflict with Egypt, culminating in the battle of Qadesh (c.1274 BC), after which the two superpowers of the Bronze Age signed a peace treaty.

The 14th and 13th centuries BC was a golden age for Hittite imperial power and culture, which is most strongly revealed in the design of their capital. A great number of buildings that can be seen here today, as well as the formidable 3.3km long defensive wall of the Upper City, were erected during this period. Although Muwattalli II (c.1306–1272 BC) made an attempt to move the capital into Tarhuntasha (a city still awaiting discovery) his son and successor Muršili III returned it to Hattusha, where it remained.

The King's Gate in the Upper City of Hattusha viewed from the ramp. On the right there was an outer wall with a tower just opposite the gate. Just imagine how vulnerable the enemy must have felt finding themselves under the fire brought to bear upon them from the massive towers by the gate and the outer wall.

The defensive strategy on the borders of the Hittite Empire directly depended on who were their neighbours. To the north and south-west were turbulent tribes who never completely submitted to Hittite rule. Therefore, chains of fortress-cities, such as Alacahöyük, were built to protect the roads leading to the capital. In case of more civilized neighbours, such as Egypt to the south-east and Arzawa to the west, Hittite rulers installed vassal principalities to act as buffer states.

This golden age did not last. Towards the end of the 13th century BC years of poor harvests, uprisings and invasions by the 'Peoples of the Sea' led to the decline of the Hittite Empire. Additional fortifications were erected in Hattusha and the grain supplies were barricaded within a separate citadel on Büyükkaya. However, this did not save the capital and, in c.1180 BC the last Hittite king, Šuppiluliuma II, left Hattusha with most of the population of the city for an unknown destination.

Many of the buildings in the former capital (the royal palace, temples, stretches of the fortification wall) reveal signs of destruction by fire. The royal citadel Büyükkale suffered most of all and was completely destroyed, with the streets being coated with a thick layer of charred wood and mud-brick tempered by fire. Those responsible for this destruction are unknown. Some believe that Mushki (Phrygians) incursions from the west were to blame while others place the blame upon the shoulders of the Kashkans to the north. The fall of the Hittite Empire should not be seen as an isolated event as the late 13th and early 12th centuries BC saw the fall of Troy and a number of Mycenaean cities as well as Hattusha.

After the collapse of the Hittite Empire, Central Anatolia experienced a period of decay, which is generally called the Dark Ages. At the same time several so-called Late Hittite kingdoms became established in south-east Anatolia and the northernmost part of Syria. These kingdoms saw themselves as the heirs of the Hittite Empire and Assyrian records continue to refer to them as the 'Land of Hatti'. Each kingdom was based on a well-fortified capital after which it is usually known today (Carchemish, Sam'al and others). Apart from the capital, border fortresses and fortified residences of the rulers also prove

Anatolia during the Hittite period

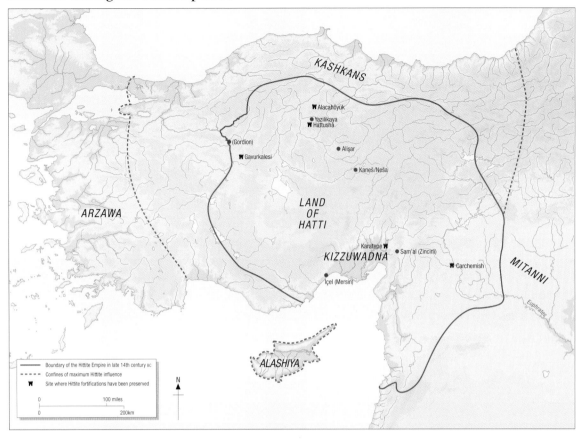

common. Karatepe proves a fine example of such a border fortress, which also served as a summer residence for the ruler. The Late Hittite kingdoms lasted to the end of the 8th century BC when, one by one, they were swallowed up by the nascent Assyrian Empire, principally between 738 and 709 BC.

CHRONOLOGY

Dating Hittite events is a far from easy matter. The main problem is a lack of established starting points. Therefore, to date an event in Hittite history one has to resort to comparison with foreign sources, often Egyptian or Assyrian. However, their chronology is not completely reliable either. To complicate matters, different Hittite kings often had the same name and are often mentioned in the documents without any indication of their succession (first, second, and so on). For instance, when we see the name of the King Tudhaliya in an inscription, we can only guess which of the four kings of the same name, covering four different centuries, is meant. Therefore, nearly all the dates cited below are approximate and may sometimes vary wildly. It should be mentioned that many different sets of dates exist with regard to Hittite chronology as well as that of other Near East countries. If the date is given with '/', it means that the date remains a subject of debate (the dates are cited in chronological order). For the kings, the years of their rule are indicated, not of their life. All the dates below refer to BC.

Hittites	Ancient Egypt	Mesopotamia	Troy	Minoan and Mycenaean civilizations
	3100/3000–2600 – Early Dynastic Period (1st–3rd Dynasties)	2900/2750–2334/2315 – Early Dynastic Period	2900–2450 – Troy I	3100–1900 – Minoan Pre-Palatial period on Crete
	2600–2181/2137 – **Old Kingdom** (3rd–6th Dynasties)	2334–2193 – Kings of Agade (Akkad)	2450–2200 – Troy II	
	2181/2137–2040 – First Intermediate Period (7th–11th Dynasties)		2200–2100 – Troy III	
		2112–2004 – The Third Dynasty of Ur (2112–2095 – Ur-Nammu)	2100–2000 – Troy IV	
	2040–1780 – **Middle Kingdom** (11th–12th Dynasties)	2000–1600 – Dynasties of the kings of Isin, Larsa, Uruk, Babylon, Eshnunna, Ashur and Mari.	2000–1700 – Troy V	1900–1700 – Minoan Proto-Palatial period on Crete
Before 1750 – Pithana and Anitta (kings of Kuššara and Neša)		1813–1781 – Shamshi-Adad I of Assyria or then the town-state of Ashur		
1740–10 – Tudhaliya I		1792–50 – Hammurabi, Old Babylonian king		
1710–1680 – Pu-Šarruma	1780–1550 – Second Intermediate Period (13th–17th Dynasties)			1700–1450 – Minoan Neo-Palatial period on Crete
1680–50 – Labarna I				
Old Kingdom (1650–1400/1350)				
1650–20 – Hattušili I				
1620–1590 – Muršili I	1650–1550 – Hyksos rulers (15th–16th Dynasties)	1595/1415–1155 – Kassite Dynasty in Babylon		1600 – Minoan influence on Cyclades
1595 – Hittites ruin Babylon				
1590–60 – Hantili I. He rebuilds and strengthens the fortifications of Hattusha				
1560–50 – Zidanta I				
1550–30 – Ammuna	1550–1085/1070 – **New Kindgom** (18th–20th Dynasties)			
1530–25 – Huzziya I				
1525–00 – Telipinu				
1500–1490 – Alluwamna	1504/1479–1450/25 – Thutmosis III			
1490–80 – Hantili II			1700–1250 – Troy VI	
1480–70 – Zidanta II				
1470–60 – Huzziya II				
1460–50 – Muwattalli I				
1450–40 – Tudhaliya II	1450–25 – Amenhotep II (Amenophis II)			1450/1400 – Mycenaeans at Knossos on Crete
1440–20 – Arnuwanda I				
1420–00 – Hattušili II				
1400–1380 – Tudhaliya III	1408/1391–1372/1349 – Amenhotep III (Amenophis III)			1400–1300 – developed fortifications appear at Mycenae and Tiryns
1400 – Hattusha is burned down by the Kashkans				
Hittite Empire (1400/1350–1200/1180)				
1380–40 – Šuppiluliuma I	1348–38 – Tutankhamun	1363–28 – Ashur-uballit I of Assyria		1380 – Destruction of Knossos
1340–39 – Arnuwanda II				
1339–06 – Muršili II				

Hittites	Ancient Egypt	Mesopotamia	Troy	Minoan and Mycenaean civilizations
1306–1272 – Muwattalli II	1306–1290 – Sety I			
	1298/90–1235/24 Ramesses II			
1274 – Battle of Qadesh between the Hittite Army of the king Muwattalli II and the Egyptian Army of the pharaoh Ramesses II		1273–44 – Shalmaneser I of Assyria		1300–1200 – Rebuilding of fortifications at Mycenae and Tiryns, construction of the fortifications in Midea and Athenian Acropolis. The golden age of Mycenaean citadels
1272–67 – Muršili III (Urhi-Tešub)			1260–50 – Destruction of Troy VIh (Trojan War?)	
1267–37 – Hattušili III				
1237–20 – Tudhaliya IV	1235/24–24/14 – Merenptah		1250–1050 – Troy VII	
	1230 – Egyptians under Merenptah rout the 'Peoples of the Sea' at the Nile delta			
1220–1190 – Arnuwanda III				1200/1800 – Widespread destruction of Mycenaean citadels and palaces
1190–? – Šuppiluliuma II	1198–66 – Ramesses III		1193–83 – Traditional dating of the Trojan War	
1180 – Šuppiluliuma II, probably together with the bulk of the city population, leaves Hattusha for an unknown destination. Hattusha is plundered by newly come tribes (Mushki or Kashkans?)	1191 – Ramesses III defeats the 'Peoples of the Sea'		1180 – Destruction of Troy VIIa	
Late Hittite Kingdoms (1180–700)				1100 – Invasion of Southern Greece by Dorian Greeks
		911–612 – Assyrian Empire		
876 – The Assyrian King Ashurnasirpal II marches through Syria to the coast. The Hittite kingdoms, following the example of Carchemish, pays a heavy tribute		883–59 – Ashurnasirpal II		
858 – United forces of Carchemish, Hattina, Bît Adini and Sam'al fail in their attempt to stop the advance of the Assyrian army of Shalmaneser III	1070–713/712 – Third Intermediate Period (21st–24th Dynasties)	858–24 – Shalmaneser III		
853 – At the cost of heavy losses suffered in the battle of Qarqar, the united forces of the kings of Hamath and Damascus stop the advancing Assyrian army of Shalmaneser III				
		744–27 – Tiglath-pileser III		
724 – Sam'al and Que annexed to Assyria		727–22 – Shalmaneser V		
720 – Hamath annexed to Assyria				
717 – Carchemish annexed to Assyria		722–05 – Sargon II		
713 – Tabal annexed to Assyria				
711 – Gurgum annexed to Assyria				
709 – Kummukhi annexed to Assyria				
	713/712–332 – Late Period (25th–31st Dynasties)	704–681 – Sennacherib		
		626–539 – Neo-Babylonian Kingdom	700–85 – Troy VIII	
		612 – The Medes and the Babylonians capture Nineveh, capital of Assyria (609 – partition of Assyria)		

METHODS OF CONSTRUCTION

Hittite fortifications, in common with many Near Eastern and Greek structures, consisted of a timber and mud-brick superstructure on a stone socle. In Anatolia, where rain and snow were fairly common, a stone socle was indispensable, as a mud-brick wall would soon be washed away without it. A timber framework gave walls additional strength, as well as resistance to the frequent earthquakes that plague the region. Mud-brick was also easy to make and it was much cheaper than stone blocks.

The stone socle of Hittite fortifications is typically constructed in a cellular manner, with the outer and inner walls divided by crosswalls at regular intervals and the cells filled with earth and rubble. The structure is sometimes called a casemate wall, which has a different meaning when applied to the fortifications of the Age of Vauban. This style is uncommon, but it is found prior to the Hittites at Alişar or Karahühük in Anatolia. The Lerna fortifications of the Peloponnese are built in the same style (Early Helladic II, second half of the 3rd millennium BC).

The various measurements of the stone socle could vary substantially. According to measurements taken on archaeological sites, the depth of the outer wall varied from 1.5 to 2.5m, while the inner wall was between 1.2 and 2.2m thick. The outer wall was nearly always thicker than the inner one, or at least the the same thickness. The size of the crosswalls also varied between 1 and 2m. The cells to be packed with earth were of a rectangular shape, 1.8–3.2m × 1.5–4.0m.

A CONSTRUCTION OF THE WALL OF HATTUSHA

The defensive walls of Hattusha are typical of Hittite fortifications. They consist of a stone socle with a timber-framed superstructure filled with mud-brick (sun-dried unbaked brick). The superstructure is surmounted with a battlemented parapet which has rounded-triangular merlons. Characteristic of Hittite fortifications is a structure consisting a stone socle of cells packed with earth and rubble. Outer and inner walls separated by crosswalls form the cells. This structure, which is known as a casemate wall, was known before the Hittites; however, it became their particular trademark.

A defensive wall near the Sphinx Gate of Alacahöyük. A perfect example of cyclopean polygonal masonry laid without any mortar. The stone blocks fit in so well that a sheet of paper could not be shoved in between them; the two blocks in the centre have been given a special projection and hollow to make them fit better.

Construction of the wall of Hattusha

Fortifications of pre-Hittite Anatolia

The best known Neolithic fortified settlement in Anatolia, and one of the most ancient in the world, is Çatal Hüyük. This settlement dates back to the 7th–6th millenniums BC and consisted of houses whose walls were built of mud-brick (sun-dried bricks) around a timber framework. There were no purpose-built fortifications, only the closely packed walls of the houses themselves, which served as a form of defensive barrier. The entrance to the houses was through the roof and no streets existed, with people walking to and fro across the flat roofs of the houses. Perhaps this primitive system of defence was most effective against floods but it proved quite adequate against unwelcome visitors armed with simple weapons as well.

As far back as the 6th millennium BC fortification walls standing away from the living quarters began to be built. The settlement of Hacilar II, dated c.5400 BC, was already protected by an independent mud-brick wall from 1.5 to 3m thick. Moderate-sized projections along the wall, resembling towers, allowed the defenders to shoot parallel to the walls. Unlike curtain walls, these tower-like projections were built on a stone socle. Some time later the settlement of Hacilar I (c.5250 BC) was protected by a more solid mud-brick wall erected in a series of 'steps', which allowed the defenders to conduct an effective flanking fire, though only on one side. In Mersin (level XVI, c.4000 BC) the fortress sat on a hill, and here already all the mud-brick fortifications were put on a terraced stone foundation. Moreover, the sloping face of the hill below the base of the wall was protected by stone slabs, which restricted access to the base of the wall. The walls consisted of more or less straight stretches interspersed with tower-shaped projections for flanking fire. The evolution of Anatolian fortifications in the 3rd millennium BC can be studied on such north-western sites as Troy I, Troy II, and Poliochni. Here a mud-brick superstructure crowned sloping rubble walls, and on the most exposed sides of the defences, the circuit-wall was strengthened with tower-shaped projections. 18th-century fortifications in Alişar consisted of a so-called casemate wall: a wall constructed of cells formed by outer and inner jackets partitioned by crosswalls. Each successive step juts out a little in comparison with the previous one resembling a saw-tooth.

The walls were then faced with huge, 2–3-ton blocks of stone – known as cyclopean masonry. The stones were laid without mortar or clay, the huge facing boulders fitted so closely that a sheet of paper could not have been slipped between them. Earthquakes have gradually loosened these structures creating gaps between them. In most cases the facing of a wall was laid with polygonal masonry. Some boulders not only fit each other perfectly but also have specially made projections and hollows allowing the stones to be joined more securely. The Hittite tradition of laying walls strikingly resembles that of the Inca.

Stone blocks were first put in the assigned place in the wall and only then was their outer surface trimmed and smoothed. Sometimes the blocks were left without the final treatment, as at the left-hand tower of the Lion Gate.

Three artefacts showing Hittite fortifications.
1. Fragment of a Hittite pottery jar from Hattusha, 15th/14th centuries BC (Hirmer Verlag, Munich). Every detail of the structure is clearly depicted: rounded-triangular merlons, windows in the tower and double timber beams protruding from under the parapet.
2. A depiction of the city of Carchemish on the Balawat Gates of the Assyrian King Shalmaneser III (858–824 BC), British Museum. Note the typical rounded-triangular merlons and the parabolic form of the gates.
3. An Egyptian representation of a Hittite city stormed by the Egyptians. Relief from the Ramesseum, first half of the 13th century BC (after S. Toy).

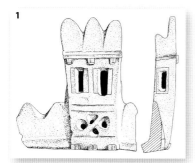

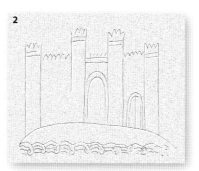

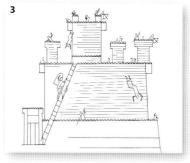

Fortifications of Jericho, Ancient Egypt and Mesopotamia

Jericho is one of the oldest, if not the oldest, fortified settlement in the world. Today its fortifications are dated back to the 8th millennium BC. The settlement was protected by a stone curtain-wall at least 7m high and 3m thick. A ditch 8m wide and over 2m deep ran in front of the wall. Even at that time a tower was raised here; 10m in diameter, it rises about 8.5m in height today. Inside this solid stone tower there is a staircase of 22 steps leading up to a fighting-platform. The amazing thing is that the tower was put on the inner side of the wall. Debates as to the function of the tower continue to this day.

The favourite material for building fortifications in Ancient Egypt was mud-brick. Walls were made from it throughout their thickness and from top to bottom without a stone socle. This was not due to the inaccessibility of stone as Egyptian temples and pyramids were built with carefully treated stone blocks. Nevertheless, the defensive walls of the same temples were made of nothing but mud-brick. For example, the famous Temple of Amon-Ra at Karnak is enclosed in formidable walls all made of mud-brick. Owing to the warm climate of Egypt, and especially the low rate of rainfall, quite a number of mud-brick fortification walls – such as those in the fortresses of Nekheb (El Kab), Nekhen (Kom el Ahmar) or Second Cataract Fortresses in Nubia – have survived to this day. Mud-brick is not a solid material and such a wall could be destroyed with a common pick. Therefore mud-brick walls were considerably thick, 3m and more. Upper parts of walls do not survive as a rule, but the height of the walls must have varied from 5 to 10m, seldom higher. Stone defensive walls were erected only in exceptional cases. An example of this is the low outer wall of the Temple of Ramesses III at Medinet Habu. A battlemented parapet with semicircular merlons closely resembling Hittite merlons can be seen on the southern reconstructed stretch of this wall. The internal, higher wall of the same temple is built entirely of mud-brick. A gate in a mud-brick wall was built of stone and was usually of a most primitive structure having a horizontal lintel or, less often, looking like a stone gate-tower.

Mud-brick was also extensively used in building fortifications in Mesopotamia, but stone was used more frequently here, both in combination with mud-brick and alone. In the little settlement of Tell Maghzaliyeh, dating back to the late 8th or the early 7th millennium BC, fortifications consisted of a stone socle about 2m high crowned with a mud-brick superstructure. The socle is built from huge stone slabs, some of them as big as 1.5m across. On the southern side the wall has a horseshoe-shaped projection 5m in diameter, possibly the foundation of a tower. A massive gate built of huge stone slabs is located on the western side of the settlement. Mud-brick fortification walls surrounded Ur at the time of Ur-Nammu (2112–2095 BC). The capitals of Assyria – Ashur, Nimrud and Nineveh – were also protected in a similar manner. Ashur was fortified with a mud-brick wall sitting on a stone socle. The wall was 6m thick and presumably 15m high. Every 20m the wall was fortified with square towers projecting beyond the wall line. A double wall – a stone outer wall and a mud-brick inner one – surrounded Nineveh. The latter was the stouter of the two and was 10m wide and 24m high. Sennacherib (704–681 BC) who erected that fortification referred to it as 'the wall that terrifies the enemy'. The circuit-walls extended for 12km with a 40m-wide ditch in front of them. At short intervals the stone wall was strengthened by narrow square turrets. Reconstructed Assyrian fortifications as well as Babylonian ones have stepped pyramidal merlons as a rule.

On rocky ground no foundation was needed for the walls. The Hittites just cut beddings in the rock to fit great stone blocks into them. In order that stone blocks stayed firmly in place, they were fixed to the rock with dowels. Holes for dowels, as well as beddings in the rock, can be seen at the north-west site of Büyükkale where the fortification walls as such have been preserved, though in a bad state. Dowels were also used for fastening the superstructure – a timber frame construction filled with mud-brick – to the stone socle. Occasionally dowels were used to fasten one stone to another, and stones joined by this method have been found at Hattusha and Alacahöyük. This form of join appears to be more common at religious sites where a great deal of care was taken in construction due both to the nature of their role and the fact that there was considerably less work involved in building a temple than constructing a fortification wall several kilometres long. The finished superstructure of a fortification wall was probably faced with plaster, as was the case with temples.

Unfortunately, due to the meteorological conditions of Anatolia, unlike in Egypt, all the mud-brick fortifications have been washed away over time leaving only the stone socles remaining, a situation much like the Mycenaean fortifications and Troy VI.

Fortifications of Bronze Age Greece and Troy VI

The earliest fortified settlements in Greece appeared towards the end of the Neolithic period. Dimini and Sesklo in Thessaly are some of the earliest and they were fortified in the 4th millennium BC. It appears that the inhabitants of the settlements relied on the number of fortifications rather than on the strength of each wall. Thus, Dimini, set on top of a hll, was enclosed by at least six circuit-walls at a distance of 1–15m from one another. The thickness of the walls (from 0.6 to 1.4m) as well as their hypothetical height (from 2 to 3m) were fairly insignificant, and the hope was placed in exhausting the enemy who would have to take several walls one after another. The walls were built of rough slate set in clay. They conformed to the contour of the hill and had no towers.

The most interesting fortifications of the Early Bronze Age, or 3rd millennium BC, are Cycladic sites such as Kastri, Phylakopi and Lerna. At Kastri the fortifications are represented by a double circuit-wall. The outer wall is all built of small flat fieldstones without any clay binding, the style resembling that of building with bricks. The wall is but from 1.0 to 1.1m thick. The inner wall, which was probably higher, is 4.5 to 6.5m apart from the outer wall. It is built in the same style, but it is stouter, with a thickness varying from 1.4 to 1.6m; it is strengthened with horseshoe-shaped towers at 4.5 to 8m intervals.

At Lerna in the Peloponnese the fortifications consisted of a fairly low stone socle and a mud-brick superstructure. Horseshoe-shaped towers projecting about 3.7m beyond the wall gave additional strength. Of particular interest is the structure of the socle. It consists of two parallel fairly delicate stone walls joined by cross-walls every 4–6m. The outer wall is 0.8–0.9m thick, the inner one 1.1–1.3m, the cross-walls are 0.9–1.0m thick. The socle is built of untreated rubbles arranged in a rare herringbone pattern; the stones are bonded with clay. The resultant cells were filled with clay. The wall was very strong and thick (4.5–5.0m). This form of construction is very similar to Hittite fortifications.

A distinctive feature of Mycenaean citadels of the Late Bronze Age (Mycenae, Tyrins and others) synchronous with the Hittite Empire is the so-called cyclopean masonry. The term cyclopean masonry is commonly used with reference to the style of building with huge unworked or slightly worked stone boulders that weigh several tons. Later Greeks believed that none but a one-eyed Cyclops had strength enough to handle such immense boulders, hence the name. The stones were laid without mortar or clay, with the space between boulders being filled with small stones. The wall was of composite construction with the hollows between the inner and outer layers of megalithic masonry being filled with rubble and earth. The thickness of such a stone wall could reach 8m or more. This stone foundation was crowned with mud-brick superstructure with a battlemented parapet. Gates were usually of a simple construction with two vertical stanchions and a horizontal stone lintel above them. Gates were often reached by a ramp and protected by towers. On the whole, however, there were few towers in Mycenaean fortresses, not more than two or three as a rule. More often than not these were not towers even but projections that did not rise above the height of the curtain wall.

In Troy VI the fortifications consisted of a thick high stone foundation with a mud-brick superstructure on top. The substructure was built on a roughly treated stone blocks of moderate size laid without of mortar. Larger pieces were used in building the bottom of a wall, smaller pieces for the top. When the erection of a wall was completed, its outer face was given a relatively smooth finish from bottom to top, which hindered escalading and presented a polished appearance to the wall. The outer face of the stone wall in Troy VI was slightly inclined inside as distinct from the strictly vertical walls of Mycenaean fortresses. The walls of Troy VI were provided with vertical offsets varying in depth from 10 to 30cm and placed regularly at intervals slightly over 9m. These offsets, occurring as early as in Mersin, level XVI (c.4000 BC), allowed the walls to slightly alter the direction without the use of corners, which were often a weak spot in fortifications. The substructure had the average thickness of about 4.8m and, in some places reached 5.25m in height. A mud-brick superstructure was strengthened by a timber-framed construction. The superstructure has not been preserved, but the hypothetical entire height of the walls could have exceeded 9m. Archaeology gives no answer to the question of what the parapets in Troy VI or Mycenaean fortresses looked like, but it is commonly believed that they were crowned with merlons of a rounded triangular shape. The gates leading to Troy VI were built in a wall next to a tower or in a corridor between overlapping walls, also under the protection of a tower. Today only three towers have been discovered in the walls of Troy VI.

The Yerkapi Rampart viewed from a rock outcrop over a ravine that was once filled with a river. The exit from the underground tunnel can be seen in the centre of the photograph; the Sphinx Gate was immediately above it on the rampart. Without the rampart it would have been easy to see the interior of the city from this rock.

Two tower-like pedestals that were possibly used as altars. Found in Carchemish, they date back to the 9th–8th centuries BC. They can be seen in the Museum of Anatolian Civilizations in Ankara today. The pedestals differ from each other in the shape of merlons: they are rounded on the left-hand pedestal and more or less rectangular on the right. The latter is not typical of Hittite fortifications of the earlier period. Also the distance between the merlons on both 'towers' is uncommonly long. It is noteworthy that the parapet with merlons is shown on both pedestals as projecting a little over the lower parts of the towers.

Archaeology is unable to tell us what the upper part of a wall built of timber and mud-brick looked like. Fortunately, artefacts exist that help us in reconstructing the appearance of this superstructure. Most important is a clay representation of fortifications that adorns the rim of a large pottery jar found in Hattusha, which dates from the 15th/14th centuries BC. Depicted on it are a tower and a small piece of curtain wall. Owing to this little clay fragment, we know that the parapet of Hittite fortifications was constructed with rounded-triangular merlons. Also clearly visible are loopholes in the tower and the ends of double timber beams protruding from under the parapet of the tower, as well as a bit below the level of the parapet of a curtain wall. Most probably these protruding beams correspond to the floors of the tower: they are not shown in the wall section illustrated.

An exterior view of the Lion Gate at Hattusha. The gate is flanked by sculptures of lions to which it owes its name. It consisted of two portals covered by parabolic arches. Rectangular towers projected on both sides of the gate to provide flanking fire.

Further scraps of information can be obtained from Assyrian and Egyptian artefacts and remains. There is an image of Carchemish on the Balawat Gates of the Assyrian King Shalmaneser III (858–824 BC). Although this is not particularly detailed, it clearly shows rounded-triangular merlons and parabolic gates. There is also a very stylized Egyptian representation of a besieged Hittite city in the Ramesseum. It shows two lines of defence and the citadel. The walls are crowned with merlons and strengthened with towers. The most interesting detail in this representation is the protruding upper section of the walls and towers as if they were overhanging the lower parts. Possibly the parapet of the towers did protrude, albeit not as prominently as shown in this Egyptian representation. There is also a small cylindrical projection, visible on the towers in the fragment of a pottery jar from Hattusha, the representation of Carchemish on the Balawat Gates of Shalmaneser III and on two pedestals-altars from Carchemish dating from the 9th–8th centuries BC. This projection of the tower parapet must have rested on the timber beams of the upper floor. We can only guess whether it had openings for missile weapons or whether objects could be dropped from them as in the manner of medieval timber hoardings or stone machicolations. In the Egyptian representation the city's defenders appear to be only shooting above the merlons.

ANATOMY OF HITTITE FORTRESSES

Hittite fortifications, like most other fortification systems of the period, are made up of a series of walls, towers and gates. A feature peculiar to the Hittites was the use of underground tunnels generally called posterns. Ramparts are not characteristic of the Hittite fortification style, although they were used occasionally.

Walls

Unfortunately, nowhere does a Hittite defensive wall survive to its full height. Today all that can be seen is the stone socle, and that much reduced, with the mud-brick and timber-frame superstructure completely destroyed. The heights of walls are therefore the matter of some conjecture; however, it is probable that the lower, stone part of the wall was about 3 or 4m high, while the upper section, including the battlements, was probably the same height again. Thus the full height of the wall apparently reached 6 or 7m. The overall thickness of the composite wall, judging by the stone socle, was about 8m on average, occasionally a metre more or less.

In the most vulnerable places, for example on the southern side of the Upper City in Hattusha, the Hittites sometimes built a double wall with the inner wall higher than the outer one. The latter stood about 7.5m apart from the former and was much thinner, no more than 1 or 2m thick. It was simple in structure, just a stone base surmounted with a low mud-brick superstructure.

The walls were probably reached by means of towers, as no stairs or ramps on the inner side have been discovered. A path would often run along the wall, providing for a quick movement of the troops in case of danger.

Towers

Hittite fortifications – even those of the Old Hittite Kingdom and Hittite Empire – are marked by a large number of towers. They considerably outnumber the towers in contemporary Mycenaean citadels or at Troy.

ABOVE AND LEFT:
Exterior and interior views of a reconstructed stretch of the defensive wall of Hattusha. The fortifications consist of a timber and mud-brick superstructure on a stone socle.

In Hattusha, for example, the towers were put close to one another, at intervals of only 12 to 30m, strengthening the wall all along its length and not only at the most vulnerable locations. Towers projected far beyond the line of the wall, providing for effective flanking fire. They were rectangular, often nearly square in shape.

If the wall was a double one, as on the southern side of the Upper City in Hattusha, the towers of the outer, lower wall were placed midway between the towers of the inner wall.

As in case of the walls, the height of towers can only be guessed at. They were undoubtedly higher than the walls – a fact confirmed by Egyptian and Assyrian images as well as a fragment of a vessel in the shape of a defensive tower with a curtain wall. However, towers owed their height more to the mud-brick superstructure rather than the stone substructure, and the latter seems to have only been as high as that of walls. The towers were presumably about 10 to 12m high, three or four metres higher than the wall itself.

According to a clay image of a tower on a fragment of a pottery jar from Hattusha, Hittite towers had three storeys. The first, ground floor was built half from stone, half from mud-brick. It was as high as the curtain-wall and had neither windows nor loopholes. The first storey towered over the curtain wall and had doors leading out onto the wall-walk as well as rectangular windows for shooting. They were just windows, not slit loopholes we see in

The best-preserved lion sculpture at the Lion Gate in the Upper City of Hattusha. The accuracy and vivacity of the image are striking: the lion had the mane and moustaches and his eyes were brightened with multicoloured stones. The stone block behind the lion is provided with a horizontal groove to accommodate the hubs of wheeled transport.

medieval castles. As no throwing machines were then known, the windows were clearly assigned exclusively for archers. Their great width may be accounted for by the material they were built of – it is not easy to make a slit with mud-brick. On the fragment there are two windows on the frontal part of the tower and one on each side. The sideward windows project out beyond the line of a curtain wall, so they were undoubtedly made to provide flanking fire along the walls. It is not clear whether there were any windows on the inner sides of towers. The second storey was just a flat fighting platform with a battlemented parapet.

A door set in the ground floor provided access to the towers. The remains of these entrances have been discovered in the basements on the inner side of some towers. Communication between storeys was possibly carried on by means of wooden stepladders.

Gates
Most of the gates of Hittite cities had a similar structure and consisted of exterior and interior portals divided by a small chamber. The arches of both portals usually had a parabolic shape, but sometimes a simple horizontal lintel formed an overhead cover, as at the Sphinx Gate in Hattusha. The gateway at the basement of an arch was usually 2.9 to 3.3m wide and about 5m high. There were exceptions though. In the above-mentioned Sphinx Gate in Hattusha the gateway of the exterior portal is 2.45m wide, while in the interior one it is only 1.7m wide.

Gates themselves normally consisted of a pair of wooden leaves locked with a heavy bar. Apertures for a bar can still be seen in the side walls of some gates (for example in the Lion and King's Gates in Hattusha). It is interesting that both sets of doors (in exterior and interior portals) opened into the gate-chamber.

Large rectangular towers (about 15 × 10m in plan) usually flanked a gate, though the Sphinx Gate in Hattusha is again unique in that it is built in a gate-tower, something very unusual in Hittite defensive architecture.

As a rule, the Hittites tried to get the enemy to approach the gate by moving along the side of the fortification wall. Steep ramps were often made for this purpose, as at the King's and Lion Gates in Hattusha or the gates of the Late Hittite fortress of Karatepe. An even more cunning system was invented for the Sphinx Gate at Hattusha. Here the enemy had to climb up one of the side stairways of the Yerkapi Rampart and then move along the wall to the gate with their flank open to the defending force.

Gates were often decorated with figures and reliefs (orthostats). Figures of lions and sphinxes were the favourites. Lions (and lionesses) were popular as talismans and gate decoration all over the ancient Near East and Mycenaean Greece – as exemplified by the famous Lion Gate of Mycenae. Hittite lions guarded not only city gates, but also entrances to some temples and the Royal Palace. The lions in reproduction always looked very much alive – with their mouths wide open and their eyes closely following the wayfarer. White limestone eyeballs with black pupils were put into the eye-sockets. Some of the lions, like those by the Lion Gate in Hattusha, had manes skilfully carved in stone. But to all appearances, the Hittites never painted the figures, they only carved them. The lions' paws rested on separate stone slabs, some of which still have bowl-shaped depressions. Travellers may have left offerings there; however, no confirmation of this has yet been found.

Sphinxes – mythical creatures consisting of a human face and a lion's body – were adopted from Egypt where they were used to represent pharaohs. The connection with pharaohs is especially transparent in the hood-like headdress falling to the lions' shoulders, where it ended in a curve. This headdress can be seen in representations of both Egyptian sphinxes and pharaohs. Most Hittite sphinxes have a similar headdress showing unquestionable Egyptian influence. At the same time, Hittite sphinxes differ perceptibly from their Egyptian counterparts. The latter are generally depicted lying while the former stand up on their paws.

BELOW LEFT
Orthostats on the North Gate of Karatepe fortress. Bilingual inscriptions in both Phoenician and Hittite hieroglyphic can be seen on the post between the reliefs and the border below. It was the bilingual inscriptions on the gates of Karatepe that allowed complete deciphering of the Hittite hieroglyphic.

BELOW RIGHT
One of the sphinxes that guarded the entrance into the Sphinx Gate in Alacahöyük. The sphinxes provide evidence of Egyptian influence. On the side of the passage the lower part of this stone block is adorned with a double-headed eagle gripping two rabbits in its claws. A female divinity, now only just identifiable, was leaning on the eagle.

The Hittites also confined themselves to showing only the front part of a sphinx as a rule, while the Egyptians showed the whole creature. Hittite sphinxes also have softer features, which leads us to assume that they represented females. The Sphinx Gate in Alacahöyük has the best-preserved sphinx. Other similar figures were placed by the outer portal of the Sphinx Gate in Hattusha and at the gate of the grand edifice in Nişantaş, also in Hattusha. The two statues of sphinxes by the inner portal of the Sphinx Gate in Hattusha are quite special. They are shown in full length with the tail twisting in a spiral at the end. They also had wings on the sides and their heads were covered with helmets, which had short cheek guards and horns at the front (a sign of their divinity).

Figures and reliefs were usually placed symmetrically on both sides of a gate. The relief on the King's Gate in Hattusha is an exception. Here it is put on the inner left-hand side of the gate. The figure has not yet been clearly identified, nor the reason for its uncommon location. Possibly, the gate was closed most of the time and opened only for religious processions.

Alacahöyük was the first place where the stone basement of the towers flanking the gate was turned into an architectural feature. The fronts of both towers had their lower parts decorated with orthostats. This method of decoration would become more widespread during the Late Hittite Kingdoms. In the fortresses of the Late Hittite Kingdoms, such as Carchemish, Karatepe or Sam'al, reliefs adorn not only the facades of the towers but also portals and gate-chambers. To make it easier for a visitor to admire them, the reliefs did not exceed 2m, and often were no more than 1m high.

An instruction given by King Arnuwanda to a mayor of the city of Hattusha has been discovered on one of the cuneiform tablets. It states that the gates of the city should be locked and sealed each night. Every morning before opening the gate the commanding officer or another official was to make sure that the seal was still intact.

Sphinxes that were once positioned by the inner portal of the Sphinx Gate in Hattusha. These differ considerably from other sphinxes in that they are shown in full, from head to tail, with wings and helmets, with short cheek guards and horns at the front. One of the sculptures is now in the Archaeological Museum in Istanbul (Ancient Orient Section), the other is in the Vorderasiatisches Museum in Berlin.

Posterns

Posterns – tunnels running under the wall and leading outside – were a distinctive feature of Hittite fortification. A number of them have been uncovered at Hattusha: one under the Yerkapi Rampart and eight in the wall between the Lower City and the Upper City, which is called Postern Wall. One tunnel-postern was discovered in Alacahöyük running under the Western Gate. While the posterns in Hattusha are straight, those in Alacahöyük are L-shaped. Similar posterns have also been discovered in Alişar, as well as in Ugarit in Syria.

The exact purpose of these posterns has yet to be discovered. They used to be thought of as sally gates through which the besieged could make a sortie and attack the besiegers to the rear. This accounts for their name – posterns. However, today this interpretation is called into question as most exits from the posterns were not disguised in any way. The outside exit from a postern under the Yerkapi Rampart in Hattusha not only lacks any camouflage, but is marked by a projecting stone extension that can be seen from a distance. Moreover, the outer exit is too far from the fortification walls for the soldiers fighting at the postern exit to get any effective fire support from archers on the walls.

The paved rampart of Yerkapi or 'gate in the earth' and the exit from the tunnel made inside this artificial rampart. This exit clearly lacks any camouflage, on the contrary it is clearly marked by a stone projection. This proves that the tunnel was in the first instance not a postern or a sally gate. Although it was possibly used for sallies in times of war, in times of peace it was designed to facilitate access into the city or serve as a passage for religious processions.

Although posterns may not have only been built for military purposes, they certainly could have been used in the case of a siege. The Hittites would have no doubt used an active defence, and not just relied on their walls to protect them. However, what would prevent a besieger from entering the city through an obvious postern? What would the point be of erecting a high rampart faced with stone and crowned with a double wall if the attackers could just break the wooden doors at the outer and inner exits of the postern and enter the city? But it is possible that the tunnels were rigged to collapse in case of infiltration by an enemy, thus proving a trap for an attacker rather than a defensive weakness.

The following fact confirms that posterns played an important role for the defenders. At the end of the 13th century BC, a second outer line of walls was built on the Yerkapi Rampart in Hattusha to strengthen the defences. This came close to blocking the Sphinx Gate on top of the rampart but the postern underneath was not blocked up and seems to have continued to function, thus emphasizing its continuous use.

The entrance and exit of a postern by the West Gate in Alacahöyük. The postern has collapsed at the exit, which used to be much closer. The tunnel turns at 90 degrees, which is untypical of Hittite posterns as they generally ran straight.

Ramparts

Some sections of the defensive walls of Hattusha stand on artificial ramparts. The most powerful of these was erected on the southern side of the city and called the Yerkapi Rampart. The rampart is 250m long and 80m thick at the base. On its outer side it is 30m high and faced with stone; the slope is

The western corner of the Yerkapi Rampart. The rampart is faced with stone and slopes at about 35 degrees. The slope can certainly be climbed up, but it was not so easy to do it under constant fire from the defenders on the two lines of walls that once towered over the rampart. On the left, just by the trees, there are steps in the rampart that lead to the top.

35 degrees. On its inner side it lacks stone facing and the slope is gentler. Some scholars believe that the shallowness of the 35-degree slope and the stairs on both sides of the Yerkapi Rampart mean that it would not have presented a serious obstacle for well-trained soldiers. Consequently, they have come to the conclusion that the paved rampart was built for decorative purposes in the first place. However, it is worth remembering that many peoples of the world have built ramparts of lesser height and designed them purely for defence. For example, ramparts in medieval Eastern Europe were rarely higher than 10m, although they were often assigned the most important role in defence. The ramparts of Yaroslav's City in Kiev, known as the highest in Medieval Rus', only reached a height of 16m with a slope of 30 to 45 degrees. Of course, it is possible to overcome a few dozens of metres up a 35 degrees slope. But it should be remembered that it had to be done under a constant fire from the walls. The attacking soldiers cannot ascend a rampart at high speed, so they present a perfect target for the enemy. A rampart had one more advantage: it prevented battering rams being moved close to the wall. Although there is no pictorial evidence of wheeled battering rams until the 9th century BC, simple hand-worked rams are known from the pictures in the tombs in Beni Hasan, Egypt, from the 21st–18th centuries BC. Battering rams are also mentioned in documents from Mari dating from the 18th century BC. Therefore, by the 14th century BC the Hittites must have had some knowledge of battering rams and taken them into consideration when building their own fortifications. There was yet another reason for the Hittites to erect a rampart on that particular side of the city. On the extreme southern end, just behind the fortification wall, a river, now dried out, ran through a hollow with a rock towering beyond it. Without a rampart, the whole of the Upper City along with the disposition of its defenders would be perfectly visible from the viewpoint of this tower of rock.

TOUR OF THE SITES: HATTUSHA, ALACAHÖYÜK AND KARATEPE

Unfortunately, not many Hittite sites can boast well-preserved fortifications today. By far the most important is the Hittite capital of Hattusha: its fortifications not only survive but long stretches have also been revealed by excavation and reconstructed. Alacahöyük was another important Hittite city, however its fortifications are as yet unexcavated. The third site examined in this chapter is Karatepe, a Late Hittite fortress that has well-preserved and

A plan of the site of Hattusha

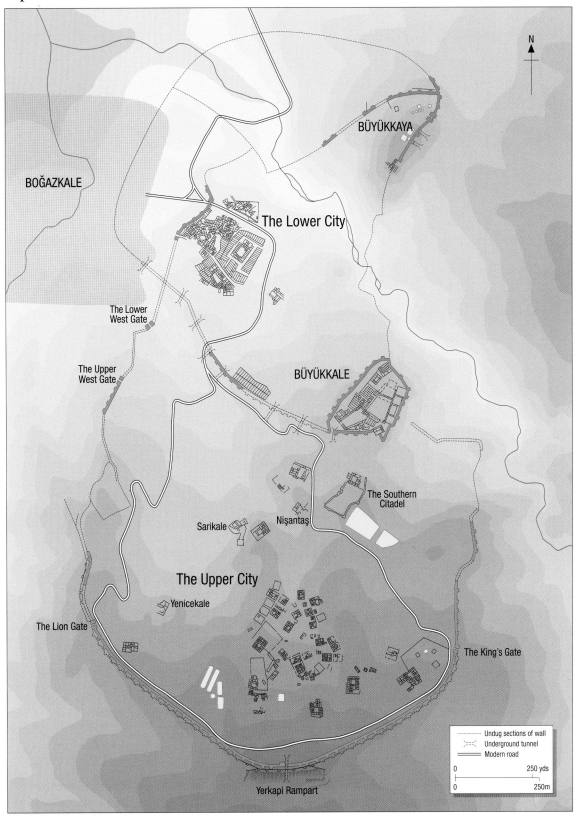

BOĞAZKALE

BÜYÜKKAYA

The Lower City

The Lower West Gate

The Upper West Gate

BÜYÜKKALE

The Southern Citadel

Sarikale

Nişantaş

The Upper City

Yenicekale

The Lion Gate

The King's Gate

Yerkapi Rampart

N

- - - - -   Undug sections of wall
⋈⋈⋈⋈   Underground tunnel
═══   Modern road

0   250 yds
0   250m

partly rebuilt fortifications. Karatepe is also easily reached as compared to other frontier fortress-cities such as Carchemish.

Hattusha

The ruins of the once-powerful Hittite city occupy a vast territory near the village of Boğazkale (former Boğazkőy). The territory falls into four fortified sites: Lower City, Upper City, Büyükkale and Büyükkaya.

The Lower City is the territory of the Old City of the Hittites. It lies to the north-west of the citadel of Büyükkale and to the north of the so-called Postern Wall. Towards the end of the 3rd or the beginning of the 2nd millennium BC, Hattians populated the Lower City, which they called Hattush. It was also in the Lower City that the Assyrian merchants' colony existed in the 19th–18th centuries BC.

One of the clay tablets discovered in Hattusha says that King Hantili I, the third king of the Old Kingdom period, who ruled in the first half of the 16th century BC, built the fortifications of Hattusha which 'earlier had no protection whatsoever'. However, this appears to be somewhat of an exaggeration, as it is now believed that the Lower City was fortified by the 16th century BC, though not anywhere near the extent to which King Hantili I fortified the site. There is no doubt that he substantially rebuilt and strengthened the defensive walls and erected new sections. The Postern Wall is believed to be one of those new sections built under King Hantili I.

The first thing that strikes a visitor of the ruins of Hattusha is a reconstructed stretch of a wall by the road leading to the entrance of the site from the village of Boğazkale. The stretch is comparatively short – just two towers and curtain walls – but it conforms to all the principles of Hittite fortification: a mud-brick superstructure surmounts a stone socle with a battlemented parapet on top. Apart from this section only the line of the Postern Wall has been traced out of the fortifications of the Lower City.

The Postern Wall forms the southern and south-western section of the defensive wall of the Lower City. It extends up to the citadel of Büyükkale and divides the Lower City and the Upper City. The Postern Wall received its name from the eight tunnels or posterns dug under the wall and leading outside. The posterns were built 70 to 180m apart from one another. Only their entrances can be seen today, the tunnels themselves have been filled with debris.

Out of the buildings inside the Lower City the following have already been excavated: the so-called Temple 1, or Great Temple, of the 13th century BC, the adjacent residential area and a two-storey house on the slope, which had a grand hall (13 × 17m) on the upper floor and served as an administrative building. The most interesting among them is certainly Temple 1, which is both the largest temple in Hattusha and the largest structure in the city. The entrance to the temple has three large thresholds flanked by small chambers for the guard. A large Inner Court, open to the air, occupies the centre of the temple. Marshalling and ceremonial assemblies took place here. From here, passing through a stoa, the king and queen in their roles as 'high priests of the land' as well as a few select temple priests, reached the innermost sanctuary, the 'holy of holies' of Temple 1. There were two cult chambers there, revealing that the temple was dedicated to two deities, supposedly the supreme deities of the Hittite pantheon, the Weather God and the Sun Goddess. A huge complex of storehouses spread out round the temple, with the lower storey alone housing 82 storerooms. At its full size, this two- or three-storey complex would have housed at least 200 storerooms.

OPPOSITE PAGE
The gate in the Postern Wall, near Büyükkale, the citadel of Hattusha. This wall divided the Lower City from the Upper City and received its name from the eight tunnels or posterns that ran under the wall.

An interior view of the King's Gate in the Upper City of Hattusha. A relief of a warrior can be seen on the left of the gate. When discovered, it was taken for a king (hence the name of the gate). Today the relief is generally believed to be the image of a god. The one shown here is a copy while the original is now at the Museum of Ancient Civilizations in Ankara.

The Upper City is the area stretching to the south of the Postern Wall up to the artificial Yerkapi Rampart. Compared with the Lower City this part of the city is new and was only surrounded with defensive walls at the period of the Hittite Empire. The length of the walls is about 3.3km.

Five gates have been discovered in the walls of the Upper City: the Lion Gate, the King's Gate, the Sphinx Gate, the Lower and the Upper West Gates.

The Lion Gate is in the south-western section of the wall of the Upper City of Hattusha. It received its name from the two sculptures of lions in front of the exterior portal. The lions were not reproduced in full stature, only snout, breast and fore-paws. They appear as if emerging from the huge stone block on the sides of the gate. The scrupulousness of the reproduction is striking and they must have made an indelible impression on the visitor. It is interesting to note that the head of the lion on the left, damaged in ancient times, was obviously bigger than that of the lion on the right. In a certain light, a Luwian hieroglyphic inscription can be seen above the left-hand lion. The inscription probably reveals the name of the gate, but only the lower character standing for the word 'gate' remains. The gate was obviously meant for wheeled transport as a horizontal groove for projecting truck hubs can be seen in the blocks of the external portal on each side of the gate. The steps on the internal side of the gate are modern. The gate was closed with heavy wooden two-leaf doors, the external ones possibly covered with bronze plates on the outside. The leaves opened inside and were locked with a wooden bar; the apertures for the bar can still be seen in the side walls of the corridor between the gates. On the outside

B **THE KING'S AND LION GATES OF THE UPPER CITY IN HATTUSHA, 13TH CENTURY BC**

Both gates had a similar structure: each consisted of two portals, exterior and interior; on either side of each gate sat two massive rectangular towers; outside the gates ran an outer, less formidable wall with a tower right opposite the gate; the gates were reached by a ramp between the outer and inner walls. The King's (1) and Lion (2) Gates resemble a mirrored reflection of each other. The King's Gate owes its name to the relief of a warrior on the inner side of the gate looking on the city. The excavators took it for the image of a king; today, however, it is more customary to consider it a representation of a god. The Lion Gate is adorned with two sculpted figures of lions placed in front of the exterior portal; hence the gate's name.

The King's and Lion Gates of the Upper City in Hattusha, 13th century BC

1

2

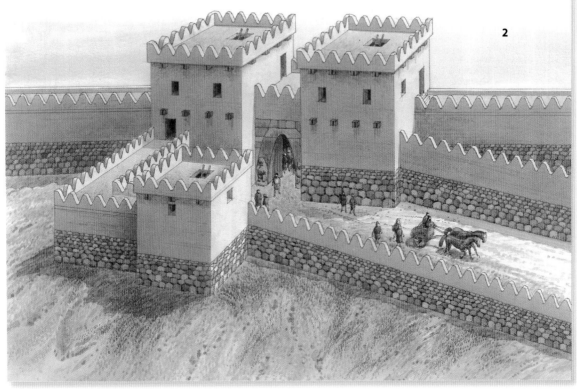

the gate was flanked by rectangular towers about 15 × 10m in plan. Fronting the gate there was another, lower defensive wall, with its tower standing right opposite the Lion Gate. The outer wall in front of the Lion Gate is insufficiently preserved and can barely be followed. However, the reconstruction on page 27 gives an idea of what the gate looked like in the 13th century BC. Any enemy wishing to seize the gate had first to fight through the gate of the outer wall. Then he would have to climb up a ramp leading steeply upward from the south to the Lion Gate. This ramp connected the outside and inside walls so here the enemy would find themselves under crossfire brought to bear upon them from both defensive lines. At last, having reached the Lion Gate, the assailants would have to struggle through the portals while being attacked to the rear by a tower of the outer defensive line and on the sides from both the flanking towers. This complex gate defence made a successful assault unlikely and would have forced any assailant to choose other sections for their attack.

The King's Gate is to the south-east of the Upper City, almost straight opposite the Lion Gate. The two gates are very similar in structure. Like the Lion Gate, the King's Gate is flanked by two towers (about 15 × 10m in plan). It also comprises two portals, an outer and inner one, covered with parabolic arches (once 5m high). They have the same system of an outer wall fronting the gate, which is reached by an approach ramp between the outward and inward walls. Stone sockets holding the pivots on which the doors swung survive at the external threshold of the King's Gate. The principal difference between the King's Gate and the Lion Gate is that the King's Gate lacks any decorative figures on the outside. As if to make up for it, there is a 2.25m-high relief of a warrior on the inside of the King's Gate. The warrior has a short wrap-around skirt on, a dagger with a crescent-shaped grip stuck at his belt and a battle axe in his hand. On his head the warrior is wearing a pointed helmet with wide check-guards, a neck-guard and horns on the sides. The helmet is adorned with a ribbon reaching down to his elbow. Today the original relief is in the Museum of Ancient Civilizations in Ankara while a copy stands by the gate. There has been some debate over the identification of the warrior on the relief; the archaeologists who had discovered it took the warrior for a king, hence the name of the gate. It is now considered to be a representation of a god due to the horns on his helmet, which are commonly used to represent deity. It is probably a reproduction of the god Šarrumma, patron and protector of King Tudhaliya IV. There still remain unanswered questions. For example, why is the relief placed on the inside of the gate, not on the outside as was usual? If it is the image of a god, could common mortals have used the gate? It is quite possible that the gate was only opened for sacred religious processions.

The Lower and Upper West Gates are similar in their structure as well as in lacking any relief or works of sculpture. Both the gates were situated in the western wall of the Upper City, both were flanked by towers and had two doorways originally built as parabolic arches. The Lower West Gate stood just over a path that led up out of a valley nearly parallel to the Postern Wall. The Upper West Gate lay further uphill and served as an entrance to the high ridge on the west of the Upper City, an area that has not been investigated by archaeologists as yet.

Most interesting was the construction of the fortification by the Sphinx Gate. The gate was put on the southernmost point in the fortification of the Upper City and stands on a large artificial rampart. The rampart was faced with stone on the outside, and every 21m there were gutters for draining rainwater from the top of the rampart down the side of the slope. The rampart was called Yerkapi, which means 'gate in the earth'. This name derives from an underground tunnel-postern running right under the Sphinx

C NEXT PAGE: THE YERKAPI RAMPART AND THE SPHINX GATE, 13TH CENTURY BC

This, the highest and southernmost point of the fortification of the Upper City of Hattusha is a construction of unique design. Yerkapi or 'gate in the earth' is an artificial rampart named after the underground tunnel (1) dug in its thickness. The purpose of the tunnel is unclear. It was once believed to be a postern for making a surprise sortie. However, the exit from the tunnel is not camouflaged, so this idea has been abandoned. Right above the tunnel was the Sphinx Gate (2), named after the four sculpted sphinxes once placed at the outer and inner portals. The gate was in a gate-tower, not in the wall between two towers as was usual. To get to the gate one had to go up one of two flights of steps placed symmetrically on either side of the rampart, then along the edge of the fortification wall. As far back as the early 13th century BC there was only one line of fortifications running on top of the rampart. Towards the end of the 13th century BC, however, a second, lower outer wall with towers was built, probably because of a growing threat to the city. This wall blocked both flights of steps and the Sphinx Gate, which were no longer used. The reconstruction of the fortifications of the early 13th century BC is shown at (3) and the reconstruction of the late 13th century BC at (4).

The Yerkapi Rampart and the Sphinx Gate, 13th century BC

Added Soil

Natural Ground Level

1

Gate. The tunnel is 71m long and from 3 to 3.3m high. It is the only postern in Hattusha open to visitors today. The tunnel had certainly been built before the rampart was erected, not cut through the latter. The tunnel was faced with stone and is a perfect example of corbelled masonry: each successive course of blocks projects a little on the inside forming a pointed vault ending with a wedge-shaped keystone. The floor of the tunnel was covered with white coating that reflected the scant light from the ends of the tunnel to allow limited visibility. The tunnel closed on both sides with two-leaved wooden doors.

The rampart was crowned with a defensive wall interrupted by the Sphinx Gate in the middle, just above the postern. The structure of the Sphinx Gate is uncharacteristic of Hittite architecture. Instead of being flanked by two towers, the gate was built in the centre of a gate-tower. The gate owed its name to the four statues of sphinxes flanking, in pairs, the outer and inner portals. The sphinxes were not alike. The ones on the outside were made in the typical Hittite manner and were more relief than sculpture, with only the head, breast and fore-paws carved out of a huge boulder. As for the sphinxes by the inner portal, they were complete pieces of sculpture reproduced from head to tail and sporting wings. The outward sphinxes were faced away from the city, while the inward ones looked towards the interior. Only one sphinx, standing by the outer portal, can be seen by the gate today, it lost its partner in ancient times. The sphinxes from the inner portal were moved into the Archaeological Museum in Istanbul (Ancient Orient Section) and the Vorderasiatisches Museum in Berlin.

In order to get to the Sphinx Gate, one had to climb up one of the two flights of steps made on both sides of the rampart. The eastern stairway has 102 steps, the western one 81. After climbing one of them, one had to walk along the wall as far as the gate. A flight of steps instead of a ramp at the gate shows that only pedestrians used this gate. But even pedestrians were rather hard put to it having to climb up such a long flight of steps. There is another interesting fact: only the outward portal of the Sphinx Gate closed with a two-leaf door. The inward portal had no door and always stood open. Taken together with the fact that the sphinxes of the inward portal faced the city, it suggests that this was not a common gate. Like the King's Gate, it is possible that only priests used it for religious ceremonies. In this case, the rampart might have also served as a gigantic platform on which the priests, and maybe the statue of a god too, were clearly visible to the spectators standing below.

Originally there was only one line of fortifications on the top of the rampart. Later on, towards the end of the 13th century BC, another line of fortifications was built outside the main wall, probably in the face of a growing threat to the city. The second wall was thinner and lower than the main one and its towers were placed opposite the curtains of the inner wall. These two levels of defence would have allowed simultaneous fire to be brought to bear upon the attacking enemy. The outer wall blocked the stairs on both sides of the rampart rendering the Sphinx Gate inaccessible. In order to build the outer wall two towers of the main wall had to be dismantled and stone was also taken from the facing of the rampart.

A few more interesting building complexes have been discovered through excavation in the Upper City: the temple district, Sarikale, Yenicekale and Nişantaş.

The temple district occupied the southern part of the site of the Upper City, just behind the Yerkapi Rampart. Thirty temples have been discovered

here, and there is a strong possibility that more are as yet undiscovered, bringing to mind the phrase 'the thousand gods of the Hatti-Land'. The Hittites did have a great number of gods – if not thousands then at least several hundred. The cult centre of Hattusha housed the temples of the main deities, both of the city itself, as well as of the other cities of the Empire. If there was no possibility of raising a temple to a god, then it was honoured with at least a sacred stone, a sacral tree or sacral grove or fountain. Temples varied greatly in size and layout but all of them had the same main features as the Great Temple in the Lower City. An entrance portal led into an open courtyard from which, through an open stoa or portico, one or more antechambers opened onto the adytum where the cult statue of the deity stood. The great number of rooms in the temples shows that they were also used for the preparation and storage of raw materials and food products; some rooms even performed an ambassadorial function for the land and people whose deity they represented. By the end of the 13th century BC the cult centre had accumulated houses and workshops alongside the temples. It is quite probable that a growing threat from their neighbours forced the population from outside the city to within the protection of the city walls, thus developing the temple district.

Sarikale, Yenicekale and Nişantaş are rock projections once crowned with buildings erected for an unknown purpose. They were very probably the same 'rock-crest houses' that are often mentioned in Hittite texts in connection with the cult of the dead. At the same time, the summits of all those rocks were fortified and, in case of the enemy penetrating the Upper City, they could be turned into islands of defence, thus hampering enemy attempts to obtain complete control of the city.

Sarikale ('yellow fortress'). A structure apparently related to the cult of death crowned this rock, towering 60m over the valley. A wall studded with towers and one gate protected the only accessible approach up the gently sloping south-eastern side. In Byzantine times the complex, including the fortifications, was rebuilt and converted into a palace.

Sarikale, which means 'yellow fortress', is a rock with steep slopes on all sides but the south-east. It was on this gently sloping side that the cult complex on the rock summit was strengthened with fortifications comprising towers and a gate.

Yenicekale, or the 'new fortress', is a rocky outcrop with its summit levelled out and fitted for the building of a complex whose purpose is still unclear. Only the foundation of the walls and a small cistern still remain. The complex was much smaller than that on Sarikale, but both of them seem to have been assigned for the same purpose. The complex was enclosed in cyclopean walls, with some of the stones weighing as much as two or three tons. The defensive wall follows the bends of the rock and there are depressions for the blocks made in the rock. In some places the preserved wall is 7m high.

Nişantaş, or Nişantepe, is another rock outcrop in the Upper City. The rock got its name (Nişantaş means 'marked rock') owing to a long inscription in Luwian hieroglyphics discovered on one of the slopes. The inscription is 8.5m long and comprises 11 lines. Unfortunately, it is badly weathered and the text has not been fully deciphered. It is only clear that the inscription was

RIGHT

In the central upper part of the photograph are the remains of the viaduct that once led from the Upper City to the main gate of the citadel of Hattusha, Büyükkale. It is the stone base of the viaduct that can be seen here today. The stone base was surmounted with a high mud-brick construction that had wooden paving for horse-drawn carts on top.

BELOW

The southern side of Büyükkale or 'great fortress', the citadel of Hattusha. The citadel served as a royal residence and contained a presence chamber and private apartments for the king. Just by the steep slope of the rock one can see the remains of rectangular towers projecting beyond the line of the walls.

made during the rein of Šuppiluliuma II, the last of the great kings of Hattusha. In the inscription the king supposedly tells the reader of his achievements, such as a victory in a sea battle and the seizure of Cyprus (known to the Hittites as Alashiya) and the building of a monument to his father (Chamber B of the rock-cut sanctuary of Yazilikaya). The top of the rock was once crowned with a grand cult edifice with a gate strongly resembling the exterior of the Sphinx Gate at Yerkapi. In front of the gate there were also statues of sphinxes, fragments of which were discovered in 1991 and are now displayed in the museum garden in Boğazkale.

Büyükkale, or the Great Fortress, is a relatively flat plateau about 250 × 140m in size. Steep slopes on all around its perimeter make it an ideal place to put a citadel. The site was populated as far back as the 3rd millennium BC, but it was the Hittites who gradually turned it into a well-fortified citadel with a royal residence. The architectural remains that can be observed here today mostly date from the period of the Hittite Empire (late 13th century BC) with some later (mainly Phrygian) additions.

Büyükkale is now reached by a stairway on the south-western side of the citadel. This, however, is a modern construction and during the Hittite era the main gate between the citadel and the Upper City was reached by a viaduct. The viaduct had a stone substructure (which remains to this day) surmounted by a high mud-brick superstructure. A surface of wooden planks, suitable for horse-drawn vehicles, was probably laid on top. Very little of the main gate has been preserved; under the Hittites it was a powerful and beautiful structure flanked by towers. The gateway consisted of two portals and two statues of lions, similar to those at the Lion Gate, were put on either sides of the outer portal. Apart from the main gate there were two other entrances to the citadel: one on the south-eastern side and the other next to the main gate on the south-western side. The latter connected the citadel with the Upper City. The citadel walls resembled the rest of the fortification walls of Hattusha, being strengthened at equal intervals by towers. The southern section of the wall, between the South-western and the South-eastern Gates, is better preserved than the rest of the wall.

Beyond the walls of the Büyükkale stood several buildings whose foundations can be seen today. Just behind the main gate is the Court of the Citadel Gate, the first of the four courts of the citadel. A small gate connected this court with the Lower Court of the Citadel, which was bordered by colonnaded porches or stoa as were the neighbouring structures – the Central Court of the Citadel and the Upper Court of the Citadel. On the sides of the Lower Court are buildings M, N, H, G and A, which served as residences for palace officials and barracks for the palace guard. On the left-hand side of the

A fortification wall on the northern slope of Büyükkaya. The projections correspond to closely positioned towers.

Büyükkale, citadel of Hattusha, late 13th century BC

The citadel served as a royal residence, containing a presence chamber and private apartments for the monarch. There were also living quarters for the palace officials and the palace guard, as well as two shrines. The main gate that connected the citadel with the Upper City was flanked by two rectangular towers; on either side of the outer portal stood two statues of lions. A viaduct of mud-brick on a stone foundation led to the gate; a timber pavement for horse-drawn carts covered this viaduct.

Central Court are the remains of buildings B and C, which are believed to be shrines, as well as building D, the royal presence chamber with 25 wooden pillars. Buildings E and F in the extreme northern part of the citadel were the private apartments of the king.

Büyükkaya means 'great rock' and it is an impressive rock outcrop projecting about 100m over the valley. As far back as about 4,000 years before the arrival of the Hittites there was a small settlement on the top of this site. The Hittites, however, raised powerful defensive walls there. The first walls were built in the 16th century BC and only defenced the gently sloping south-eastern side. To the north of Büyükkaya this wall joined the northern wall of the Lower City. Another fortification wall was later erected on the northern slope of Büyükkaya; it joined the wall running through the Lower City by the rock called Mihraplikaya. As a result, Büyükkaya found itself protected by fortifications on all sides except the impregnable south-western slope. The bases of these walls can still be clearly seen on the northern and eastern sides, especially viewed from the Rock Sanctuary of Yazilikaya or the approaches to it.

The view from Büyükkale onto Büyükkaya, Hattusha. There is a river flowing along the bottom of the gorge between these rocks and the Hittite defensive walls extended from one rock to the other. A bridge was thrown over the gorge at the narrowest place. But how the defence of the gorge itself was organized is still a puzzle. The river is so full in spring that it would have washed away any walls, especially those made of mud-brick. Whereas an enemy detachment could easily have got into the city along the riverbed in any other season.

The South Gate of Alacahöyük. It is also known as the Sphinx Gate owing to two sphinxes put on both sides of the gate passage. Two rectangular towers, whose stone socles were decorated with orthostats, flanked the gate, 14th century BC.

A deep ravine with a stream running along its bottom divides Büyükkale and Büyükkaya. The Hittites connected the two sides with a fortification wall that crossed the ravine at the narrowest place, near a rock projection known as Ambarlikaya. Cuttings from stone blocks embedded in the rock, as well as dowel-holes, suggest that once there was a fortified stone bridge thrown over the ravine at the height of about 15m connecting the defensive walls on either side of the ravine. This structure, however, dates from the Byzantine period. The Hittites probably had two towers here, one on each side of the ravine, connected with a simple suspension bridge for the guards. How the Hittites blocked the streambed is still a question. In spring, the water stands so high as to rule out any permanent construction, especially one made from mud-brick. In any other season, however, the streambed would be accessible to an enemy force. The stream was apparently partitioned with grilles of some kind and the ravine was carefully guarded throughout its length. If discovered in time, an enemy would be easily destroyed by fire from both sides of the ravine.

Alacahöyük

Alacahöyük had been inhabited since 4000 BC. During the Early Bronze Age it was the centre of the flourishing Hattian culture. Thirteen royal tombs dating from about 2500 BC have revealed to the world a great number of amazing artefacts created by this culture, a pre-Hittite non-Indo-European people. However, the surviving architectural remains were built during the Hittite Empire, mainly in the 14th century BC.

Under the Hittites, it was an important city lying a short way from the capital of Hattusha. It was heavily fortified against the continuous raids of the Kashka people, who regularly invaded Hittite territory and at least once captured Hattusha itself. The fortifications of Alacahöyük consisted of thick walls strengthened with rectangular towers. Unfortunately, most of these

An interior view of the North Gate of Karatepe fortress. Next to nothing has survived of the fortifications and a modern weatherproof concrete roof has been built to preserve the orthostats.

fortifications, as well as most of the city proper, have not been excavated yet. Only the general line of the walls has been traced, and the exact number of towers is still unknown. Two main gates led into the city: the West Gate and the South Gate. Not much of the West Gate survives and it is only known that two rectangular towers flanked it and an underground L-shaped postern ran below it. The South Gate is comparatively well preserved. It is commonly known as the Sphinx Gate owing to two statues of sphinxes, carved out of 4m high monoliths, which flanked the outward side of the gate. The stone bases of both towers flanking the Sphinx Gate were covered with orthostats showing the king and queen, worshipping a bull, animals for the sacrifice, priests, jugglers, etc. The orthostats are copies, the originals having been moved into the Museum of Ancient Civilizations in Ankara.

Karatepe

Karatepe, which means 'black mountain', is a Late Hittite fortress founded in the 8th century BC by Asatiwatas (or Asitawada), the Hittite king of Adana. The fortress served as either a royal summer residence or a frontier outpost. It did not remain long in service as the Assyrians seized it and burnt it to the ground in either 720 or 680 BC.

A substantial amount of the curtain wall has been reconstructed to a considerable height. The walls are laid from rough medium-sized stones, with the core consisting of earth mixed with rubble. The mud-brick superstructure has not been reconstructed, so the walls look unfinished.

The fortress had two main gates – the South Gate and the North Gate. They are very similar in structure and resemble the Lion and the King's Gates in Hattusha. The gates are flanked with formidable towers on either side and fronted by an additional wall and a tower to form a barbican. Thus, the gates were protected against a direct attack: the enemy could only reach the gate by passing the wall and one of the towers and then taking a 90-degree turn to the left. They would then find themselves in an extremely unfavourable position – under a crossfire from the gate, the flanking towers, and the tower and wall of the barbican. The gateway itself comprises an outer and inner portal with a corridor in between opening onto two rooms to the side.

41

Tower of Karatepe fortress. The high stone socles for walls along with towers reconstructed and preserved by archaeologists can be seen here today. A mud-brick superstructure crowned by a parapet with merlons sat on top of this.

Both the gates are richly decorated with orthostats on the exterior, as well as all along the gateway. The reliefs depict scenes from everyday live, hunting scenes, religious activities, a war ship, warriors, etc. The North Gate was flanked by sculptures of lions; right behind the South Gate a 3m-high statue of the weather god stood on top of a double bull socle. Of most value, however, are the inscriptions on the orthostats. These are bilingual inscriptions in Phoenician and Hittite hieroglyphic. As the Phoenician language had already been deciphered, these inscriptions allowed the decoding of the hieroglyphic form of the Hittite language. The inscriptions, made in the first person, glorify the deeds of King Asatiwatas.

The gates have not been reconstructed except for the orthostats, which have been placed on either side of the gateway. Ruins of a palace and granaries have been discovered in the fortress, all of which were destroyed by a fire.

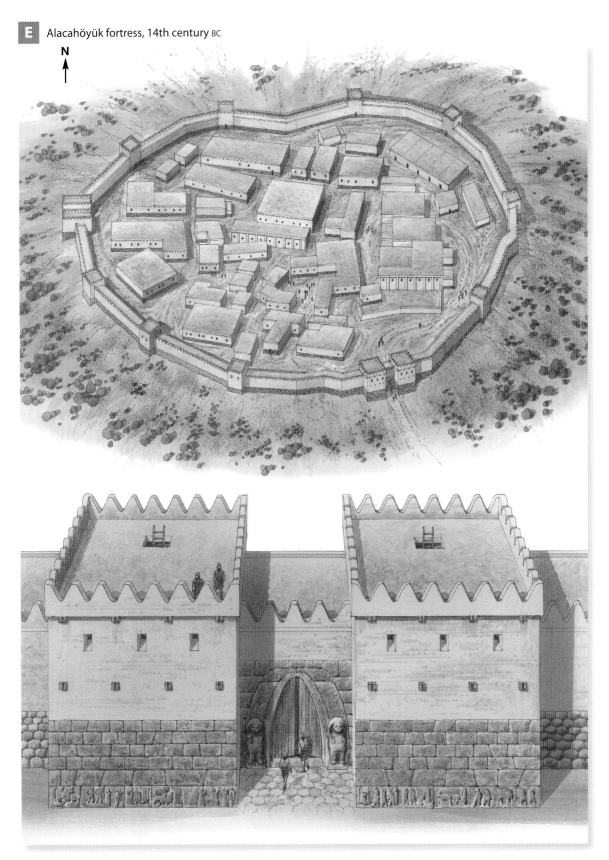

E Alacahöyük fortress, 14th century BC

SANCTUARIES AND THE LIVING SITES

Religious activity formed a central part of Hittite life in common with many other ancient peoples. Places of worship were the most significant civil buildings, and temples and sanctuaries have survived in an incomparably better state than the houses of ordinary people. The Hittites had a great number of gods; modern researchers have counted several hundred of them while the Hittites called their country 'a land of a thousand gods'. Numerous reliefs representing gods and goddesses survive in the territory of the former Hittite Empire. Among them the Rock Sanctuary of Yazilikaya is particularly impressive: while in other places single figures or at best isolated groups of figures of deities are shown, in Yazilikaya we find a whole gallery of more than 80 such figures.

Rock Sanctuary of Yazilikaya. The holy of holies of this sanctuary consisted of two chambers (A and B) in the open air. The sides of both chambers in the rock were carved with reliefs of gods and goddesses. Chamber A is in the top photograph, Chamber B is in the bottom one.

44

Yazilikaya means 'written rock' and the site is situated about 1km north-east of Boğazkale (Hattusha). The site was in use from the 15th century BC but it was only in the second half of the 13th century BC, under King Tudhaliya IV, that the figures of gods and goddesses appeared here and Yazilikaya was transformed into a religious complex whose remains survive to this day.

The Rock Sanctuary of Yazilikaya comprises two rooms called Chamber A and Chamber B. In front of the entrance into the sanctuary there was an impressive complex of one-storey buildings characteristic of the Hittites: a stone socle surmounted with mud-brick walls and a timber framework. The entrance was on the left and a visitor was first to pass through a gateway of stairs. Then another set of stairs led him out into an open court. Here ablutions and preliminary rites were performed, confirmed by the presence of an altar. Right behind the altar there was a third staircase that took the visitor up into Chamber A. Only the ruins of the stone basement have been preserved from the complex of buildings in front of the entrance.

Chamber A is the larger of the two chambers and is about 30m long. Its walls are adorned with 66 figures of gods. A procession of male deities (with two exceptions) can be seen on the left; a female procession is shown on the right. Both processions are moving towards the opposite end of the chamber where the main event is depicted – the meeting of the leaders of the two processions, the Weather God Teshub and the Sun Goddess Hebat. The male figures are wearing short skirts and high pointed caps with one or two horns at the front (a headdress characteristic of gods), their shoes curls up at the toe; many of them are armed with an uncommon weapon with a curved blade or a mace (these weapons are clearer on the figures in Chamber B). The female figures are dressed in long pleated skirts and wear curl-toed shoes, earrings and high headdresses. Not only are the male and female figures dressed differently, but they are also depicted in a different way, which is typical of Hittite art: the females are shown strictly in profile, while the males have their faces in profile and their torsos turned towards the observer.

On climbing a few steps on the right of the entrance to Chamber A, the visitor finds himself in a narrow passage that takes him into Chamber B. The passage is guarded by two winged lion-headed demons. Chamber B is considerably smaller in size, about 18m long and 2.5 to 4m wide. The reliefs are much better preserved here as the chamber was partly filled with earth. It is very probable that Chamber B was a memorial to the King Tudhaliya IV and was erected by his son Šuppululiuma II. A 3m-high statue of King Tudhaliya IV,

A relief from Chamber B in the Rock Sanctuary of Yazilikaya depicting a procession of 12 male deities armed with an unusual weapon with a heavy curved blade.

2

N

1

This is the most interesting of the Late Hittite fortresses accessible to visitors today. King Asatiwatas built it as a summer residence or a border outpost, or possibly for both purposes. The fortress could be reached by two main gates, the South (1) and the North (2). Both were protected by two formidable towers on either side and an outer work consisting of a wall with a tower. Immediately beyond the South Gate stood a 3m statue of the principal Hittite deity, the Weather God.

An image of the god Nergal of the underworld – a dagger, driven into the ground, its handle made in the shape of two lions with its pommel forming a male head. Chamber B, Rock Sanctuary of Yazilikaya.

which does not survive, supposedly stood here. On the right of the entrance a relief can be seen representing 12 gods of the underworld identical to a group of 12 gods in Chamber A. The opposite wall is decorated with three reliefs: the god Sharrumma striding forwards with the King Tudhaliya IV under his arm, a cartouche with the name and title of the King Tudhaliya IV and the 'Sword God'. The last relief is quite unique, showing an upright dagger with a ribbed blade sharply narrowing towards the cutting edge. Two lions with their mouths open, portrayed vertically, form the hilt of the dagger. The pommel is made in the shape of a male head wearing a tall pointed horned hat characteristic of gods; below the head there are the foreparts of two crouching lions. In the region of Diyarbakir a bronze dagger has been discovered with two opposing lions on the hilt. A cuneiform inscription dates the object back to the Old Assyrian period and establishes that it was a votive offering to the temple of the god Nergal of the underworld, which leads to the assumption that the unique relief in Chamber B also represents the Nergal of the underworld.

The reliefs were undoubtedly more distinct at the time of the Hittites than they are now. When created they would have had an almost white surface contrasting with the grey surface of the rock. Moreover, the reliefs were most probably painted, although no trace of this survives. They have different illumination depending on the time of day or year. In Chamber A the male deities are clearly visible in the late morning, the goddesses are better seen in the early afternoon. The relief on the back wall showing the meeting of the main gods is best seen between 2 and 4pm. Chamber B receives the best light from 11am to 1pm.

Neither of the chambers with reliefs was ever roofed but remained open to the sky. The Yazilikaya Sanctuary probably served as a place for the celebration of the arrival of the Hittite New Year each spring.

Yazilikaya was an unfortified sanctuary. There were, however, also fortified sanctuaries. For example, Gavurkalesi ('the castle of infidels') was fortified with a cyclopean wall. Today most scholars believe that the Gavurkalesi complex served religious purposes, though it used to be considered a king's tomb.

Gavurkalesi is situated on top of a rock towering about 60m over the surrounding valley. It is a Hittite monument

Gavurkalesi. Relief representing three figures: a seated one to the left (hardly discernible because of erosion) and, on the right, two figures moving towards the first. The left-hand figure is supposed to represent a goddess while the right-hand ones are the Weather God followed by his son. The three figures together are a trio of father, mother and son. The remains of cyclopean masonry fortification can be seen on the right just behind the relief.

dating from the 14th century BC. On the southern side on the flattened face of the rock there is a relief showing three deities: a seated figure of what is supposedly a goddess to the left (now hardly distinguishable owing to erosion), and two male figures moving in her direction to the right. Both the males are carrying daggers with T-shaped hilts in their belts and wearing conical helmets decorated with a ribbon that reaches down to the elbow. The foremost male figure has three horns on both front and back, while the other one's helmet has three horns only on the front. On the whole, the equipment of the figures closely resembles that of the warrior relief on the King's Gate in Hattusha. Ekrem Akurgal thinks that the male figures represent the Weather God followed by his son, and all the three figures together constitute a trio of father, mother and son.

Entrance into a small (about 3 × 4m) underground chamber in Gavurkalesi. The purpose of this chamber, as with the whole Gavurkalesi complex, is unclear. Some scholars consider it to be a royal burial chamber, others believe it to be a place of worship.

Gavurkalesi. The remains of a Hittite fortification wall made of huge andesite blocks without mortar. Most of the stone blocks are 120–150cm long and about 50cm high.

On the northern side right opposite the relief there is an entrance to a small underground chamber (about 3 × 4m) laid with cyclopean stone blocks.

A cyclopean wall built with andesite blocks, mined only a kilometre away, protected the entire summit of the hill of Gavurkalesi. A substantial stretch of the wall can be seen today to the east of the relief. Stone blocks were placed without mortar and on average they are 120–150cm long and 50cm high. There are the remains of another defensive wall with towers in front of the relief, dating supposedly from the Phrygian period. This wall was constructed of white limestone, with smaller stones that those of the Hittite wall. Their average length is 80–100cm and their height is 50 to 90cm. The wall is as thick as two rows of the stone blocks.

The living sites

The populations of these cities consisted of the nobility, priests, merchants, artisans and civil servants. Peasants lived in villages or close to the city, but not inside the city walls.

Two types of houses were characteristic of domestic architecture: courtyard houses, with an open courtyard, and vestibule houses, with a roofed-over living area. Houses with open courtyards were more typical of the earlier period, while fully roofed ones came into fashion later. House walls were made of mud-brick supported by a timber frame construction. The roofs were flat, wooden and covered with mud. Water for everyday needs had to be brought in buckets; however, some of the houses were furnished with sewer pipes carrying waste away to purpose-built drains beneath the streets.

Grain was stored in special granaries dug below ground. These granaries were rectangular cellars and either paved (as in Büyükkaya) or laid with stone on all sides (as in Alacahöyük). Eleven of these cellars have been discovered in Büyükkaya, though there would certainly have been more. The largest granary, 12 × 18m and 2m deep, could contain at least 260 tons of grain. When all the cellars were filled, even a major city such as Hattusha could withstand a siege of several years. To prevent the grain from deteriorating, the cellars were

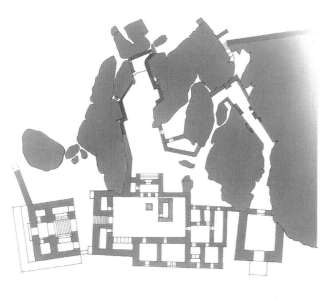

G THE ROCK SANCTUARY OF YAZILIKAYA, SECOND HALF OF THE 13TH CENTURY BC

This unique sanctuary housed the images of about 80 gods, goddesses and King Tudhaliya IV, who was probably responsible for the creation of this place of worship. The sanctuary consisted of two chambers in the rock, Chamber A and Chamber B, as well as an impressive complex of buildings in front of them. Having performed ablutions and preliminary rites at the altar, a visitor moved to the larger Chamber A where before him, right on the walls of the rock, he would see two processions, one of gods on the left and that of goddesses on the right. The processions were heading for the distant wall of the chamber where the encounter between the leaders of the two processions – the Weather God Teshub and the Sun Goddess Hebat – is depicted. The smaller Chamber B was also adorned with reliefs showing gods; it was probably a memorial to King Tudhaliya IV erected by his son Šuppiluliuma II.

Granary in Alacahöyük. The granary was divided into rectangular cellars lined with stone on all sides. A cellar could contain up to several hundred tons of grain.

covered with a thick layer of soil, which sealed the grain in protecting it from pests and preventing decay. This method of storage could keep grain fresh for years and is still used in parts of Turkey to this day.

Water was usually stored in cisterns, sometimes so large that they could be more properly called reservoirs. For example, near the Southern Citadel in the Upper City of Hattusha two reservoirs have been discovered. The one that has been fully excavated is *c.*60 × 90m, while the other appears to be similar in size. The banks of these reservoirs were laid with stone with the

Artificial pond 1 by the walls of the Southern Citadel of Hattusha. The extent of the pond is shown by the line of stones forming the edge. Its bottom, however, was unpaved and only covered with a watertight layer of clay. The pond was at least 2m deep.

A small artificial pond near Alacahöyük formed after the construction of a dam. The stone dam that can be seen in the distance is one of over 10 built by the Hittite King Tudhaliya IV in the 1230s BC to save the country from drought. A canal connected the pond with the city and supplied its water for everyday needs. In 2002 the dam was rebuilt and the inhabitants of the village of Alacahöyük now use the pond for irrigation purposes.

bottom left unpaved as the underlying rock proved to be practically waterproof, requiring only a layer of clay. These reservoirs were fed by several springs, one from the Upper City and others from outside the city walls. The water travelled along clay pipes, one of which passed through the fortification wall below the King's Gate.

Five more reservoirs have been discovered on a height in the southern part of the Upper City in Hattusha. One is small and round, the others are narrow and elongated and reach a depth of 8m. The soil is almost watertight here, so no special methods were used to safeguard the water supply. Through a system of clay pipes and canals, the reservoirs were filled with water coming from springs in the southern part of the city. Other clay pipes carried it away to various parts of the Upper City. The reservoirs were probably built in the 15th century BC. The reason why five reservoirs were constructed instead of just one large one is unknown.

Near the city of Alacahöyük the Hittites constructed a dam that created a small reservoir. This was connected to the city by a canal that supplied the city with its everyday needs.

Some information about the nature of the garrisons of these Hittite fortifications can be picked up from clay tablets that have survived. From these it has been discovered that garrison service was one of the duties of the Hittite army and that during times of peace the troops were billeted in the fortresses to make up their garrisons. A garrison could consist of regular Hittite troops, detachments of vassals or allied kings, as well as recruits specially enlisted for this service. It seems that in their major cities Hittites preferred to man a garrison with those from outside the area rather than with local population.

When they campaigned in enemy territory the Hittites left strong garrisons in newly captured fortresses. Their purpose was to guarantee the loyalty of the local population as well as to maintain military pressure on the enemy.

Even in enemy territory, Hittite garrisons only consisted of a few hundred men. For example, one of the Old Hittite texts says that towards the end of a campaign the garrison of the city of Tipiya consisted of only 300 men, even though the city was one of the three that were to serve as a base for the next year's campaign. When Muršili II seized the state of Mira, making it a tributary province, he built three fortresses and left a garrison of 600 men apparently distributed between them. These troops were to serve as "watchmen concerning the person (of the king of Mira), because the people of Mira are treacherous"[1].

Garrison troops were called *ašandula/i-*, with the same term being applied to troops used offensively in siege fortifications as well as those used in outposts established to pacify enemy territory. In another source the term *gurtawanni-* (derived from the word *gurta-* meaning 'fortress') is used, but it is unclear whether it means castellan, an inhabitant or defender of a fortress.

AFTERMATH

Many Hittite cities were reoccupied after a short period of neglect. The Kashkans, who may well have been one of the parties responsible for the fall of the Hittite Empire, moved into former heartland of the Hittites. The Kashkans constructed their buildings out of timber and, as wooden buildings built without foundations and not set on posts leave no noticeable marks in the soil, their dwellings have both disappeared without trace and left the underlying Hittite monuments intact. To the west the Mushki, known as the Phrygians in the Greek tradition, moved into the territory. The Phrygians migrated from Macedonia and Thrace to Asia Minor either before or after the Trojan War. There is no clear archaeological evidence about the Phrygians before the mid-8th century BC, and the most detailed information relates to Phrygia's prosperity under King Midas. Gordion, the capital of Phrygia, lay on the western border of the former Hittite Empire and important Phrygian settlements have been discovered in the former Hittite cities of Hattusha and Alacahöyük as well as at other sites.

Hattusha saw the most significant development by the Phrygians, who called it Pteria. The 8th century BC saw the development of a large settlement that occupied Büyükkaya, Büyükkale and part of the Lower City. In the early 7th century BC the threat of a Cimmerian invasion caused a population shift and spurred the Phrygians to build new fortifications. The settlement on Büyükkaya was abandoned, the citadel on Büyükkale was encircled by new fortifications and a new fortress, today called the Southern Citadel, was built 100m south of Büyükkale.

Plan of Büyükkale during the Phrygian period (after K. Bittel). Phrygian structures are marked with thick lines, Hittite ones are shown with thin lines. Note how much higher the north-western Phrygian wall is than the Hittite one. On the south-western slope of the hill the Phrygians erected a bastion as well as a round structure nearby, probably for cult purposes.

1. Beal, R. H., *The Organisation of the Hittite Military* p. 234.

The south-western corner of the Büyükkale Royal Citadel. The staircase was built in modern times. The main gate of the citadel had been reached by a viaduct, the remains of which can be seen alongside the asphalt road to the right. The remains of the south-western bastion, a Phrygian tower resembling bastions of the Age of Vauban, are in the centre of the photograph, by the stairs in the hill slope.

From the 8th through 6th centuries BC, the Büyükkale plateau was thickly built over by the Phrygians. Numerous fairly small structures now occupied the territory that once housed courts with colonnaded porches, residences of palace officials, temples and royal apartments. This rebuilding work was carried out to such an extent that only the experienced eye of an archaeologist can tell Hittite buildings from Phrygian ones. Old Hittite fortifications on the southern and eastern sides had seemingly suffered insignificant change and were reused. But the north-western side acquired a new defensive wall with towers that ran closer to the summit of the hill than the Hittite one. The walls of the Hittite buildings H, E and F served as a foundation for this new Phrygian wall. The new location of the western wall made it necessary to change the south-western corner of the citadel. The western wall was connected with the southern one, with the junction lying a distance inside the Hittite main gate. The Hittite gate was destroyed and a new one erected a little further to the north. Structurally the new gate resembled the old Hittite one but it had a longer and narrower entanceway. Not content with this, the Phrygians built yet another gate on the south-eastern side, close to the location of the Hittite Southeast Gate. At first, the new gate was just a simple gateway cut in the wall,

A double-tier socle of the Southern Citadel, Hattusha. The Phrygians built the citadel in the 7th century BC, probably as defence against the Cimmerians. A mud-brick superstructure, apparently similar to a Hittite one, crowned the stone socle. The masonry at extreme left corresponds to the facing of artificial pond 1.

but a single tower later flanked it. This was eventually rebuilt to consist of two portals with two sets of doors and a spacious chamber between them. Artificial oblique ramps led to all of the gates.

A tower projecting a considerable distance beyond the line of the walls was built in the south-west corner of the citadel on the slope of a hill. Owing to this projection, the tower provided the Phrygians with excellent flanking protection along the entire length of the southern and south-eastern slopes. The tower had a pentagonal shape – unusual for that period – which greatly resembled the bastions of the fortifications of Vauban.

The Phrygians covered the southern and south-western slopes of Büyükkale with a pavement of limestone from foot to the top. Not only did this lining hamper any attempt by an enemy to scale the slopes, but it also prevented erosion caused by rainstorms and melting snow. The stone lining of the slopes was renewed more than once, which emphasizes its significance to the Phrygians. They apparently got the idea for slopes lined with stone (glacis) from the Hittites, as the Yerkapi Rampart was probably paved in this manner. On the whole, this kind of glacis was characteristic of 7th–6th-century fortifications from central and northern Anatolia, and in Göllüdağ near Niğde it was used as far back as the 8th century BC. Later examples are known in Cappadocia and in the Pontic area (at Kerkenesdağ, Havuzköy and Akalan).

In the 6th century BC the Phrygians built a long staircase on the western slope of the citadel. It led outside the defensive walls to a well. As the well was located beyond the normal bowshot range from the fortifications, a detached square tower was built close to it for protection. A similar system of water supply has been uncovered in Midas City, which implies that this was a Phrygian defensive tradition.

The Phrygians re-used a large number of the high-quality Hittite stone blocks, destroying a large number of Hittite structures on Büyükkale. For example, the north-western Hittite fortification wall almost completely disappeared, with its stone used to erect the new Phrygian wall up the hill.

A massive (over 4m thick in places) socle of quarrystone survives of the fortifications of the Southern Citadel of the 7th century BC. The socle is surmounted with another, narrower socle also made of quarrystone. On top of this foundation there seems to have been a mud-brick superstructure with

Wall of the Southern Citadel, Hattusha, viewed from inside the city. The grating in the centre of the photograph hides the Hieroglyph Chamber built in early-12th century BC by the last Hittite king of Hattusha, Šuppiluliuma II. The chamber is supposed to have served as a symbolic entrance to the underworld. In the 7th century BC the Phrygians used stones from the chamber to erect the walls of a citadel. Today, however, archaeologists have completely restored the inner decor of the room, including the reliefs of the Sun God and King Šuppiluliuma II, as well as an inscription in Luwian hieroglyphics.

timber insets, as was common in Hittite fortifications. Irregular in plan, the fortress walls were strengthened with towers. These structures were rectangular and jutted out slightly beyond the line of the walls, resembling projections of the curtain wall rather than towers proper. The corner towers, on the other hand, were structurally similar to the south-west bastion of Büyükkale. They markedly projected beyond the wall line, with their pointed corner facing the enemy. The only gate, flanked by two towers, was on the north-western side of the fortress.

By the Byzantine period most of the Hittite cities had been long abandoned. However, there were some Byzantine developments. A sizeable Byzantine settlement is known to have existed in the 10th–11th centuries on the site of Hattusha to the south-east of Sarikale, while on Sarikale itself a Hittite cult building was rebuilt and strengthened with new fortifications to become the palace for a local Byzantine ruler. It seems to have been the Byzantines who were responsible for the disappearance of one of the sphinxes at the Sphinx Gate. The statue was probably used as building material. The same fate was apparently in store for its counterpart as it was found already dismantled and broken into pieces. Deep chiselled grooves were found on the reverse side of the block, which were characteristic of the Roman and Byzantine practice of splitting larger blocks into smaller ones. It escaped destruction by sheer chance and now adorns the Sphinx Gate in Hattusha.

Some of the sites have been preserved by archaeologists, such as the granaries of Büyükkaya that have been filled in after excavation to keep them safe. However, many of the ruins have suffered in present times, with the stone still being used for local construction work. A striking example of this can be seen is the village of Zincirli, situated on the site of the citadel of the once-powerful city of Sam'al. Judging by the numerous ditches dug by archaeologists in the late 19th century, as well as detailed plans and reconstructions, the excavations should have revealed a great number of foundations for fortifications and palace structures. However, not a single stone can be seen on the site today. At the same time, the local houses and fences are constructed out of stone, often from the massive stone blocks that were used to line the ancient walls; Hittite reliefs can even be seen on some of them.

THE SITES TODAY

Alacahöyük

The site is about 180km east of Ankara, near the highway D785 to Çorum (about 30km from the town) and 35km north-east of Hattusha. Close to the archaeological site there is a small but interesting museum where some of the excavated artefacts are displayed. However, the most valuable discoveries such as magnificent gold and bronze objects from Hattian Royal tombs or the original orthostats that once adorned the Sphinx Gate, are in the Museum of Ancient Civilizations in Ankara.
Open: Tue to Sun, from 8am to 5pm, with a break from 12 to 1pm.
Tel.: (+90 364) 422 70 11

Alişar

About 60km south-east of Yozgat and about 15km from Sarikaya lies the village of Alişar; two kilometres from Alişar, beyond the highway, hidden under a hill, are the ruins of a settlement that existed both in pre-Hittite and Hittite time. Only a few trenches crossing the hill can be seen here today.

Carchemish

The site is on the very border between Turkey and Syria, about 60km south-east of Gazi Antep (Turkey) and 100km north-east of Aleppo (Syria). Unfortunately, a Turkish military base now occupies the citadel of Carchemish so access is heavily restricted. A part of the ancient city may be located on Syrian territory, but because of the frontier location excavations have been partial.

The city controlled an important ford across the Euphrates and its strategically advantageous position ensured the city's prosperity over the years. The site had been inhabited since the Neolithic period and Carchemish

One of the orthostats decorating the stone socle of the gatehouse of the Sphinx Gate at Alacahöyük. The relief shows jugglers: the one on the left is swallowing a dagger, the one on the right climbs a ladder that stands up in the air. Alacahöyük can now boast only copies as the originals are displayed in the Museum of Ancient Civilizations in Ankara.

General view of Gavurkalesi. On the right-hand part of the hill is a vertical slope with the famous relief showing three Hittite deities. Right behind it is the surviving section of Hittite cyclopean fortifications, while in front of it are the ruins of a later wall, probably of the Phrygian period.

is mentioned in the Ebla (3rd millennium BC) and Mari (2nd millennium BC) archives. In middle of the 2nd millennium BC the city was one of the centres of the kingdom of Mitanni and in the 14th century BC it was seized by the Hittite King Šuppiluliuma I and became one of the most important centres of the Hittite Empire. After the fall of the empire, the city became the capital of the Late Hittite Kingdom. The peak of its prosperity fell in the 11th century BC, followed by a period of decay and, by 990 BC, a small city-state was based upon it. Nevertheless, it remained independent up to 717 BC when the Assyrian King Sargon II conquered it. In the summer of 605 (or 607) BC a famous battle between Babylonian and Egyptian armies took place by the walls of Carchemish.

Archaeological excavations undertaken by the British Museum between 1911 and 1914 revealed substantial remains of the Late Hittite and Assyrian periods, including fortifications, palaces, temples and numerous basalt reliefs. The latter are displayed in the Museum of Ancient Civilizations in Ankara today. The city was enclosed with three defensive lines and consisted of the Outer City, Inner City and the Citadel, the latter backing onto the river. The uncovered walls of the Inner City were 5.8m thick and had external and internal vertical offsets.

Gavurkalesi or Gavurkale ('the castle of infidels')

The site is near the village of Dereküy, which can be reached by highway 260 connecting Ankara and Haymana, a town south-west of Ankara. The distance from Ankara to Gavurkalesi is about 50km, from Haymana about 10–15km.

Hans H. von der Osten excavated Gavurkalesi in 1930 and suggested that it was an isolated fortified hilltop monument. A religious building and houses for priests were supposed to have stood on the top, protected by cyclopean walls. If it was so, the buildings were completely destroyed in the following centuries. The only survivors are a stretch of cyclopean wall and a mysterious chamber whose purpose is unknown. Excavations in Gavurkalesi and within the surrounding valley in 1993 made it clear that the monument on the top of the hill was not an isolated structure. Apparently it was more complex and accompanied by some type of settlement.

Hattusha (Hattuša, Hattuşaş or Hatush)

The ruins of the former Hittite capital are to be found near the village Boğazkale (which means 'gorge fortress'); the village was once called Boğazkőy ('gorge village'). The nearest big city, Yozgat is 37km away. Boğazkale can be reached from Ankara either on highways E88 and D200 through Yozgat (about 230km) or on highways E88 and D785 (about 180km). There are several lovely small hotels in Boğazkale. In high season, however, they can get very full.

Hattusha is one of the most attractive archaeological sites in Turkey, one of its nine sites included in the World Heritage List (UNESCO).

The site occupies a vast territory and had better be investigated in a car as an asphalt road winds between the sights. If you are travelling on your own and have no car, a taxi can be hired in Boğazkale. A comprehensive guide to the site is available.

A lot of the artefacts discovered during the excavations in Hattusha are now displayed in a small local museum in Boğazkale and in the Çorum Museum in the town of Çorum (82km away, highway D785). Both museums are certainly worth visiting. It is quite easy to get from Boğazkale to the Rock Sanctuary of Yazilikaya (1km) and to Alacahöyük (35km).

Information on Hattusha:
Open daily, except Monday, from 8am to 6pm.
Tel.: (+90 364) 452 20 06

Içel (Mersin)

Excavations at Yumuk Tepe, 3km west of the city, exposed remains of fortifications of the Old Hittite Period. The excavated section of a wall with towers is classical in structure, it comprises outer and inner walls divided at regular intervals by crosswalls. The artefacts dug out in the course of the excavations are displayed in the Adana Museum.

Kaneš/Neša (modern Kültepe)

Kültepe ('hill of ashes') is about 20km north-east of Kayseri, near highway D260 Kayseri–Sivas. It is one of the best-known Bronze Age sites in Turkey. The ancient name of the city that was once the capital of a kingdom of the same name is Kaneš (or Kanesh). The site was inhabited from the 4th millennium BC and has four building levels, the last of which appears in two phases (Ib and Ia).

The site comprises two parts: the mound 500m in diameter and 20m high and an Assyrian merchant colony (kârum) that occupied a territory of about 1,500 × 1,000m on the eastern side of the mound. Some other cities of Anatolia, for example Hattusha in the pre-Hittite period, also housed an Assyrian merchant colony but kârum Kaneš was the largest to which all the other kârums were subordinate. It was encircled by a city wall and Assyrian merchants lived there for centuries

TOP: Plan of a stretch of urban fortifications, Old Hittite period, Içel (Mersin) (after J. Garstang). Like other classical Hittite fortifications, this wall comprises outer and inner walls, divided at regular intervals by crosswalls.
BOTTOM: Section of the city wall at Alişar (after von der Osten). It is a pre-Hittite wall (18th century BC) also consisting of cells but lacking towers. Instead, it is built in a series of 'steps' resembling saw-teeth, which seems a less successful arrangement.

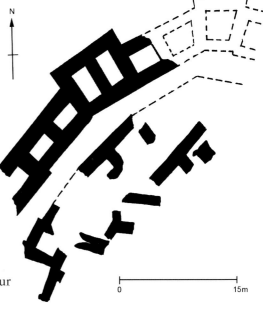

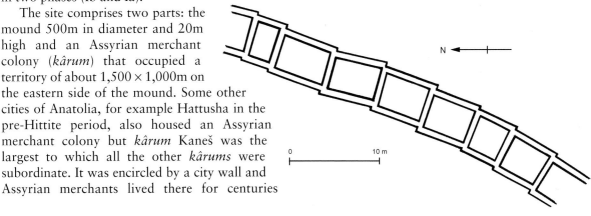

Wall of Karatepe fortress near the South Gate. The site is in a picturesque park on the shore of Lake Aslantaş, which can be seen on the right in the photograph. Several picnic areas in the park attract numerous tourists, even those indifferent to Hittite history.

exchanging local goods for goods from Assyria and Elam. The site of Kültepe is famous for the discovery of numerous clay tablets (about 15,000) found there. The tablets mostly reflected common activities such as trade and legal arrangements. They are the earliest written Anatolian documents.

The Assyrian trading colony existed here from about the early 20th century BC to the mid-18th century BC, which corresponds to levels II and Ib. In both levels a significant quantity of ashes has been discovered, which points to the destruction by fire of the site on two separate occasions (mid-19th and mid-18th centuries BC). After the first fire it remained deserted for about 40 or 50 years but then it was populated again. After the second fire the colony was abandoned permanently.

The same is not true of the mound. In the age of the Assyrian merchant colonies it was the residence of the kings and the nobility of the kingdom. Excavations have revealed palaces forming an impressive complex with wide courts, large halls, long corridors and premises for administrative functions. The palaces had plastered mud-brick walls on top of stone foundations. Citadel walls ran along the brink of the mound and had a rubble core between the outer and inner facing made of large stones. The devastating fire that destroyed the Assyrian trading colony damaged the mound too, but did not cause it to be

This hill conceals the remains of the citadel of Sam'al, the capital of the Late Hittite Kingdom, a flourishing city in the 10th–8th centuries BC. The village of Zincirli occupies the other side of the hill unseen in the photograph.

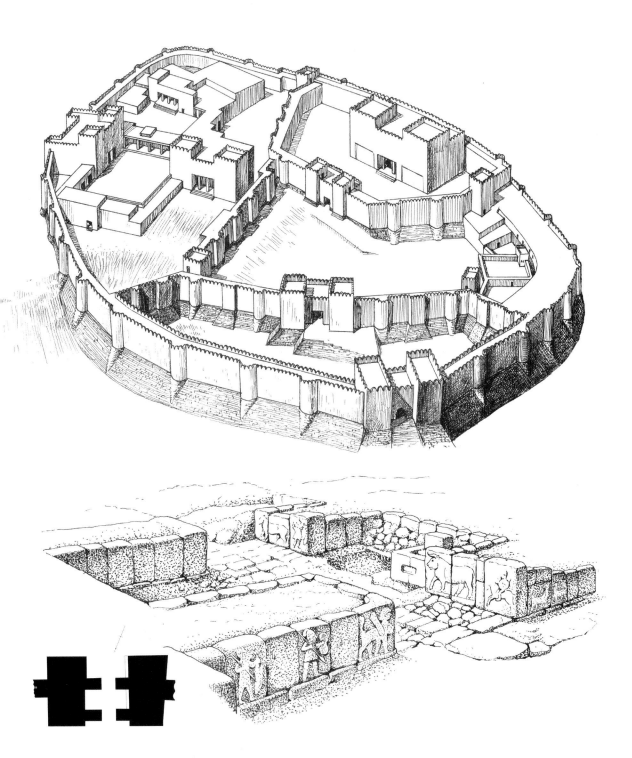

abandoned. Pithana, the first of the Hittite kings known to us, seized the city 'in the night, by force' but 'did not do evil to anyone in it'. The city fell under the authority of the Hittites, who first called it Kaneša and then Neša. Under King Anitta, son of Pithana, the city rose against Hittite rule. However, Anitta suppressed the uprising and then made Neša his capital. Even after moving their capital to Hattusha, the Hittites continued to call their language Nešili, which means 'the language of Neša'. In the Late Hittite period it became an important city in the country called the Kingdom of Tabal by the Assyrians.

Sam'al (Zincirli): reconstruction of the citadel and the arrangement of orthostats in the outer gate of the citadel. Irregular in shape, the citadel was divided with inner walls into a few fortified sites. The gate was decorated with numerous orthostats on the front as well as along the passage.

A minor part of the mound and a sector with houses and streets in the *kârum* have been excavated. Most of the fortifications, those surrounding the Assyrian merchant colony as well as those following the borderline of the mound, still lie underground. Most of the artefacts discovered at Kültepe and belonging to Assyrian, Hittite, Persian and Roman periods are on display in the Museum of Ancient Civilizations in Ankara, the rest can be seen in a small local museum and in the museum in Kayseri.

Open daily from 7am to 5.30pm.
Tel.: (+90 352) 289 32 32

Karatepe

The site is situated on a hill, on the shore of the picturesque Lake Aslantaş near the mouth of the river Ceyhan, about 30km north of Osmaniye and approximately 130km north-east of Adana. Thanks to the work of Professor Halet Çambel, this Late Hittite fortress has been converted into a charming open-air museum, which has become part of a vast park of the same name. On the opposite side of the river Ceyhan there is another Late Hittite site, Domuztepe; however, it is less impressive.

The Karatepe open-air museum is open from 8am to 4.30pm.
Tel.: (+90 328) 719 20 73 and 719 20 03

Sam'al (Zincirli)

The site is located in the modern village of Zincirli, which was built on the site of the citadel of the ancient city of Sam'al. Zincirli lies about 12km south-west of the town of Nurdağı, which in its turn is approximately 70km west of Gazi Antep.

Sam'al was the capital of a Late Hittite Kingdom of the same name that existed from the 10th century BC to approximately 724 BC when it was annexed to the Assyrian Empire. Its strategically important position at a crossroads connecting the west, the east and the north ensured the city's fast commercial growth. Excavations carried on in the late 19th century revealed powerful urban fortifications and a citadel. The urban fortifications, circular in plan, were represented by a double wall with 100 towers and three gates. The citadel was irregular in shape and divided into several courts with inner walls. Unfortunately, nothing reminds us of its former glory. The most valuable artefacts discovered here, including giant statues of lions, numerous orthostats and inscriptions in Aramaic, Phoenician, Luwian and Akkadian, are now displayed in the Archaeological Museum in Istanbul and Vorderasiatisches Museum in Berlin.

BIBLIOGRAPHY AND FURTHER READING

Akurgal, E., *Anadolu Kültür Tarihi* (Ankara, 1998)
Akurgal, E., *Ancient Civilizations and Ruins of Turkey: From Prehistoric Times until the end of the Roman Empire* (Istanbul, 1970)
Akurgal, E., *Hatti ve Hitit Uygarliklari* (Izmir, 1995)
Akurgal, E., *The Hattian and Hittite Civilizations* (Ankara, 2001)
Alp, S., *Hitit Çağinda Anadolu* (Ankara, 2001)
Beal, R.H., *The Organisation of the Hittite Military* (Heidelberg, 1992)
Bittel, K., *Die Heithiter* (München, 1976)

Bittel, K., *Hattusha. The Capital of the Hittites* (New York, 1970)

Bittel, K., *Die Ruinen von Boğazköy* (Berlin and Leipzig, 1937)

Bittel, K., 'Reports of excavations at Boğazköy', *Mitteilungen der Deutschen Orientgesellschaft*, LXX–LXXVIII (1932–9) and LXXXVI (1953) ff.

Bittel, K., and Naumann, R., *Boğazköy-Hattuša* (Stuttgart, 1952)

Brandau, B., Schickert, H., Hethiter. *Die unbekannte Weltmacht* (München, 2001)

Bryce, T., *The Kingdom of the Hittites* (Oxford, 1998)

Bryce, T., *Life and Society in the Hittite World* (Oxford, 2004)

Cavaignac, E., *Les Hittites* (Paris, 1950)

Cavaignac, E., *Le problème hittite* (Paris, 1936)

Contenau, G., *La civilisation des hittites et des hurrites du Mitanni* (Paris, 1948)

Darga, M., *Hitit Sanati* (Istanbul, 1992)

Delaporte, L., *Les Hittites* (Paris, 1936)

Dussaud, R., *Prélydiens, Hittites et Achéens* (Paris, 1953)

Garstang, J., *Prehistoric Mersin* (Oxford & New York, 1953)

Garstang, J., *The Land of the Hittites* (London, 1910)

Garstang, J., *The Hittite Empire* (London, 1929)

Goetze, A., *Das Hethiter Reich* (Leipzig, 1928)

Goetze, A., *Hethiter, Churriter und Assyrer* (Oslo, 1936)

Gurney, O.R., *The Hittites* (Baltimore, 1964)

Huxley, G. L., *Achaeans and Hittites* (Oxford, 1960)

Klengel, H., *Geschichte des Hethitischen Reiches* (Leiden-Boston-Köln, 1999)

Konteno, J., *'Khetty', Khetty i khettskaya kultura* (Moscow and Leningrad, 1924)

Macqueen, J.G., *The Hittites and their Contemporaries in Asia Minor* (Boulder, 1975)

Neve, P., *Hattusha — Information* (Istanbul, 1985)

Osten, H. H., von der, *The Alishar Hüyük. Seasons of 1930–32.* (Univ. of Chicago. Or. Inst. Publ. XXVIII–XXX, 1937)

Osten, H. H., von der, *Explorations in Central Anatolia. Season of 1926.* (Univ. of Chicago. Or. Inst. Publ. V, 1929)

Osten, H. H., von der, *Explorations in Hittite Asia Minor 1927–9.* (Univ. of Chicago. Or. Inst. Comm, 6 & 8, 1929–30)

Pritchard, J. B., *Ancient Near Eastern Texts relating to the Old Testament* (Princeton, 1950)

Rehberi, K., *Ana Tanriça Kybele'nin ve Kral Midas'in Ikesi Phrygia* (Ankara, 2002)

Riemschneider, M., *Die Welt der Hethiter* (Stuttgart, 1954)

Roaf, M., *Cultural Atlas of Mesopotamia and the Ancient Near East* (Abingdon, 2004)

Rowton, M. B., 'The Date of the Hittite Capture of Babylon', *Bulletin of the American Schools of Oriental Research*, 126, 20–4 (1952)

Sayce, A. H., *The Hittites. The Story of a Forgotten Empire* (London, 1910)

Schirmer, W., *Hitit Mimarliği* (Istanbul, 1982)

Seeher, J., *Hattusha Guide. A Day in the Hittite Capital* (Istanbul, 2002)

Sommer, F., *Hethiter und Hethitisch* (Stuttgart, 1947)

Sturtevant, E. H., *A Hittite Glossary* (Philadelphia, 1936)

Toy, S., *Castles. Their Constructions and History* (New York, 1985)

Volkov, A. V., Nepomnyaschii, N. N., *Khetty. Neizvestnaya imperia Maloy Azii* (Moscow, 2004)

Wolley, C. L., *Carchemish*. Part II. *The Town Defences* (London, 1921)

Wooley, L., *The Art of the Middle East, including Persia, Mesopotamia and Palestine* (New York, 1961)

Zakharov, A. A., 'Khetskaya kultura', *Khetty i khetskaya kultura* (Moscow and Leningrad, 1924)

INDEX